MY FATHER BALIAH

Dr Y.B. Satyanarayana hails from a poor Dalit family. He is the sixth child born to Baliah and his wife Narsamma. Dr Satyanarayana completed a master of science from Osmania University in 1971 and began teaching first at the Government Junior College, Nirmal, and then moved to a private college. At thirty-three, he became the principal of Dharmavant College of Science and Commerce, Hyderabad, a post he held until his retirement twenty-five years later. For over three decades, he taught chemistry, a subject in which he also took a PhD. As an academic, he has been part of several governing bodies, including the executive councils of Kakatiya University and Osmania University.

A staunch follower of Dr Ambedkar's teachings, he began to take a keen interest in Dalit literature and history in the early 1990s, and started studying the progress of Dalits in various fields. On 14 October 2006, along with thousands of other Dalits, he gave up Hinduism and embraced Buddhism.

He is currently the president of the Centre for Dalit Studies, Hyderabad.

MY FATHER BALIAH

Y.B. Satyanarayana

HarperCollins *Publishers* India

First published in India in 2011 by
HarperCollins *Publishers* India

Copyright © Y.B. Satyanarayana 2011

P-ISBN: 978-93-5029-075-0
E-ISBN: 978-93-5029-437-6

4 6 8 10 9 7 5 3

HarperCollins *Publishers*
A-75, Sector 57, Noida, Uttar Pradesh 201301, India
1 London Bridge Street, London SE1 9GF, United Kingdom
Hazelton Lanes, 55 Avenue Road, Suite 2900, Toronto, Ontario M5R 3L2
and 1995 Markham Road, Scarborough, Ontario M1B 5M8, Canada
25 Ryde Road, Pymble, Sydney, NSW 2073, Australia
195 Broadway, New York, NY 10007, USA

Typeset in Garamond Premier Pro 11/15
Jojy Philip, New Delhi

Printed and bound at
Saurabh Printers Pvt. Ltd.

To my father, Baliah,
and my unlettered mother, Narsamma

Yelukati Family Tree

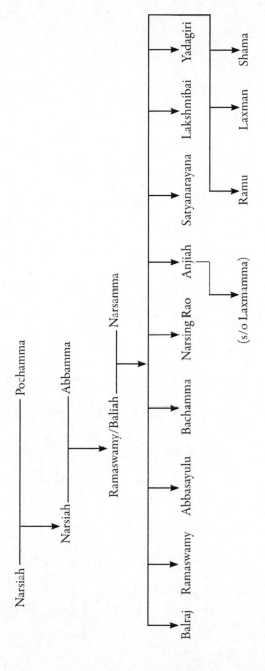

Children of Baliah alive: Bachamma, Anjiah, Satyanarayana, Lakshmibai and Laxman Rao; Yadagiri is missing

Child deaths: Ramaswamy, Ramu and Shama

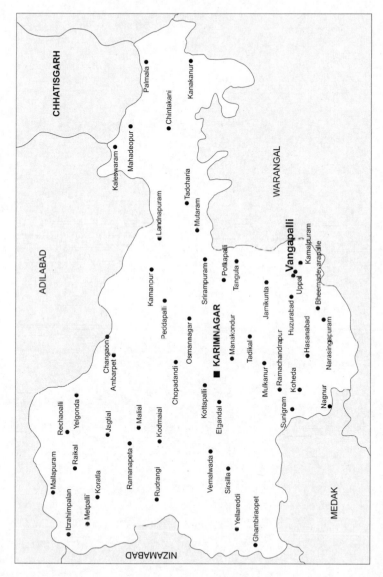

Map not to scale

Foreword

I take great pleasure in writing the foreword to *My Father Baliah* by Dr Y.B. Satyanarayana. This book is Dr Satyanarayana's tribute to his father Yelukati Ramaswamy (later known as Yelukati Baliah) and to his forefathers. This biography, introspective at times, is a vivid portrayal of the journey of a family belonging to the Dalit Madiga community of Telangana in Andhra Pradesh. It is also a history of the Yelukati family which strove for a better world against all odds. The book depicts continuity as well as change over a period of almost two centuries and three generations. But it is not merely a family chronicle. Rather, it is the depiction of the lived experiences of members of the Madiga community over several decades in different places, settings and situations, making it a unique social history of the times.

My Father Baliah is a detailed delineation of the different facets of the unique world of untouchables – the inviolable societal boundaries and attitudes, the social, economic and cultural landscapes, the norms and patterns of intercommunity and interpersonal relationships, the ways of life and means of living, the negotiations and compromises and the aspirations and shortcomings as well. The narrative becomes a history of the relentless struggle of an untouchable community against social and economic discrimination, against oppressive caste hierarchy, against feudal conditions, and against ridicule and humiliation. It brings out the inhuman cruelty of untouchability and the caste system, and the helpless acquiescence and internalization of this condition by the untouchable community itself. At the same time, the book does not fail to bring out the kindness of some people belonging to other communities, especially the deep affection and empathy shown by some teachers.

During my career as an officer of the Indian Administrative Service (IAS) in Andhra Pradesh, I had the good fortune of working among the poorer sections of the people, particularly those belonging to the scheduled castes and scheduled tribes. I have seen untouchability being brutally put into practice, despite constitutional and legal commandments to the contrary. I can even now recall the image of a Dalit woman sitting on the banks of a water tank with a pot in her hand, waiting for someone to 'pour' water from the tank into her pot, since, being an untouchable, she was forbidden from entering the tank and collecting the water herself. I have been appalled at the manner in which derogatory suffixes are attached to the names of people from the untouchable community to depict their lowly status in the caste hierarchy. I have personally seen the exploitation of bonded labourers, many of whom were bonded for generations for repayment of paltry sums taken as loans from landlords. I have seen fear writ large on the face of Dalits while in the presence of big landlords, known as Doras in the Telangana area, and have felt the intensity of social oppression denoted by the expression 'I am your slave, I touch your feet' which was the compulsory conventional salutation with which untouchables were called upon to address people belonging to the so-called upper castes. Such sufferings of the untouchable community and the indignities heaped upon them are brought out in the narrative as it describes the life history of the Yelukati family.

There is another reason for my attachment to this book. Having lived in railway colonies in my younger days, I related easily to the depiction of life in such mixed colonies where the rigours of the caste system were somewhat – though not fully – loosened. I have closely observed gangmen, pointsmen and shunters, mostly drawn from the so-called lower castes, as well as stationmasters and railway guards – mostly from the upper castes – with their 'guard boxes', and the manner in which their relationships at official and personal levels were negotiated. I have often marvelled at the 'run through' trains which sped away with someone keeping aloft the green flags on the platform. I have witnessed women rushing to collect water from the steam engines of those days, and the fact that ticketless travel by members of the families of railway staff was conventionally accepted as legitimate! Until the end of the Second World War, grain shops too were operated by the railways for railway staff. The railways constituted a universe somewhat different from the rest of the society. This book brings out all these aspects vividly in relation to the life of a Dalit family which struggled to overcome the feudal oppression in the villages. As the author observes, the railways constituted the universe for them. The author's father, who did not know much about the world beyond the railways, was firm in his view that his children should be educated well only so they could become railway officers.

The advent of British rule offered new positions in the army with the cantonments, the docks, the railroads, the mines and the mills. These provided new opportunities to people of the untouchable community. In fact, there was wide access to such jobs for untouchables since people belonging to the so-called upper castes were not ready to take them up; the jobs were difficult and hazardous, and the latter often also had inhibitions based on notions of caste pollution. It may be worthwhile recalling in this context that Babasaheb Ambedkar himself belonged to an army family and was born in Mhow, an army station. Ramabai Ambedkar too was from a similar family.

As the author rightly points out, the railways opened a route for Dalits to get out of the stifling and oppressive atmosphere of the villages by providing jobs, even though these were manual and menial. Untouchables gained entry into the railways. To live in the railway quarters along with other castes was a new and liberating experience for people who were treated as outcasts and segregated as such in every village. They found similar opportunities in coal mines too.

The story of the life of Shri Narsiah starts in a small village called Vangapalli in the Karimnagar district of Telangana in Andhra Pradesh. When the nizam of Hyderabad was on a tour through this village, Narsiah's father, whose name was also Narsiah, presented the nizam with a beautiful pair of shoes made from the hide of a young calf. The nizam was so pleased that he declared a gift of fifty acres of land to this gentleman, the great-grandfather of the author. But land, even when gifted by the nizam himself, could not be enjoyed by them because of the feudal power of the local Dora who permitted Narsiah to occupy only two acres. Strange but true that Narsiah was neither dismayed nor resentful about this turn of events, but relieved. Not sorry that the land was seized from him, but happy that he could have at least two acres and that he was also saved the wrath of the Dora! Indeed, such a situation exists even today in several villages where, even if the government grants land to people belonging to the scheduled castes, they cannot effectively occupy or cultivate it, owing to the prevailing local power dynamics.

The author gives a detailed description of the social structure of a village. His words speak to us poignantly and directly:

> Most villages in India have for centuries had the same composition. A village has the perfect Hindu caste set-up with all the characteristic features codified by Manu. It has two types of dwellings, varna houses and avarna huts, separated by either a boundary or a well-maintained distance.
>
> In order to avoid pollution (from the casteless untouchables) through wind to caste Hindus, the houses of each varna (caste) are built in such a way that the wind blows from the dwellings of the Brahmins to the rest of the village. Untouchable (avarna) houses are located in the east and the main village in the west, since the wind always blows from west to east. Houses are built in ascending

order of the caste hierarchy from east to west – Sudras, Vaishyas, Kshatriyas and Brahmins. The houses of those belonging to the productive caste (the Sudras) cluster together, and towards the east, finally, is the agraharam, Brahmins' dwellings – the 'beginning' of the village.

These words almost echo those of Babasaheb Ambedkar, who was himself extremely critical of the social structure of the Indian village, which was otherwise often held out as an example of the ideal community or a village republic. Babasaheb hit out at the false romanticization of the Indian village thus:

> The Indian village is the very negation of a republic. If it is a republic, it is a republic of the touchables by the touchables and for the touchables. The untouchables have no rights. They are only to wait, serve and submit. In this republic, there is no place for democracy. There is no room for equality. There is no room for liberty and there is no room for fraternity.

Education in the Yelukati family started against all social and religious odds. As the author mentions, it was a Muslim teacher who first sowed the seeds of learning within the Yelukati family, which had for centuries, along with all others of their community, been denied the privilege. One is deeply moved when the author expresses the gratitude of the Yelukati family to this first teacher of the family, salutes him with great reverence and asks coming generations to remember Ali Saheb forever.

Narsiah wanted to save his son from becoming a bonded labourer in the village. His migration from the ancestral village due to continued harassment by the higher castes changed the course of history, not only for his generation, but also for future generations of his family, which were thus freed from such bondage. Baliah, out of his conviction that it is from self-respect and relentless hard work alone that one derives strength, confidence and recognition, made it the mission of his life to provide good education to his children. The migration to the city and employment in the railways provided relief from feudal oppression and a degree of anonymity too. But as the narrative shows, the caste system and its attendant social stigma followed a Dalit everywhere – even into the city, necessitating concealment of caste while studying, renting out a house, or even while engaged in the office. The book emphasizes the crucial role of education as an instrument of social change and transformation. In its social potential, education becomes a process of transmitting a specific consciousness to particular social groups. Babasaheb Ambedkar too saw education not just as a means for a livelihood but as a powerful tool to liberate Dalits and strengthen their fight against injustice and humiliation.

Again, this book tells of changes taking place in different spheres of life. People from three generations of the Yelukati family worked in the railways and were witness to the transformation of the railway system over the decades, from howling steam engines to silent electrical ones, from manual signals to electric and electronic signals, and from telegraphic messages to computer programming. Likewise, changes took place in the living conditions of the Yelukati family, from the use of earthen pots to aluminium vessels, from the consumption of jowar rotis to chapattis, from a joint family organization to individual families, and other changes in lifestyle like the switch from illiteracy to education in elite educational institutions in the country and abroad.

The book is also a tribute to Dr Y.B. Abbasayulu, the author's brother, who studied by the light of a flickering oil lamp in a shed, and after matriculation, started his career as an ordinary signaller in the railways, but reached the height of his academic career as a popular professor of sociology in Osmania University.

This excellent book brings out not only the existential situation but also the inherent potential of people to struggle and succeed against all odds and obstacles. Such narratives serve as inspirations for other members of the community to use education to overcome massive social and economic impediments. It holds out hope that it is possible to work your way up the social ladder.

I consider it appropriate to conclude my foreword to this book with the inspiring message given by Babasaheb Ambedkar in April 1947 to all struggling Dalits:

> My message is struggle and more struggle, sacrifice and more sacrifice. It is struggle and struggle alone, without counting the sacrifice or suffering, that will bring their emancipation. Nothing else will.
>
> The untouchables must develop a collective will to rise and resist and must believe in the sacredness of their task and develop a common determination to achieve their goal. Their task is so great and the purpose so noble that all untouchables should join in prayer and say, 'Blessed are they who are alive to the duty of raising those among whom they are born. Blessed are they who vow to give the flower of their days, their strength of soul and body and their might, to further the campaign of resistance to slavery. Blessed are they who resolve – come good, come evil, come sunshine, come tempest, come honour, come dishonour – not to stop until the untouchables have fully recovered their manhood.'

October 2011   S.R. Sankaran

Preface

I am a retired teacher. A teacher of chemistry all along, I never dreamt that one day I would write the story of my own family, a Dalit family. This is the story of three generations of my family, and I have woven it together from the memories I have of conversations with my grandfather Narsiah, my father Baliah, my aunt Pentamma and my elder sister Bachamma. Mainly, though the incidents narrated here were recounted by my father after his retirement when, every evening, I would get him a drink and sit by his side while he told me stories about the days when he and my mother struggled to raise us.

This story tells of a journey over different places and times and lives. It moves from a remote village, Vangapalli, through various places in the Telangana region, and terminates at Secunderabad, twin to Hyderabad, the capital city of Andhra Pradesh. In temporal reckoning, it stretches over a period of great change and turbulence in Indian history – from colonial times to independent India. It is also a story of changing lives. To begin with, it tells of my grandfather who lost his parents, his wife, his land – indeed, everything except his six-year-old son – and set out on a journey to seek a family, and ultimately found shelter with his maternal uncles who lived miles away from his village. It also tells of his son, my father Baliah, and his progeny, who across three generations, moved from illiteracy to the highest levels of education that the modern system of education offers; from a hand-to-mouth existence to a life that allows for deep reflection and self-development.

At another level, this is also the story of a community. It has been my lasting desire to show the present Dalit generation – and more so the future generations – how Dalits struggled. In the early twentieth century, Dalits were outcasts and lived in wretched conditions. I have myself been witness to the practice of untouchability and hope that future generations of Dalits will be free from this evil custom. The colonial government, with its own economic considerations in mind, recruited Dalits en masse in various fields, though mainly in professions considered menial and risky, especially in the railways, and provided something that they had never enjoyed before – regular wages and common living spaces with the Sudras. This proved to be an opportunity where the Dalits (untouchables) stepped out from their segregated dwellings and started living with the Sudras. Many Dalit families, my own included, benefited much from this move. Thousands of untouchables could now gain at least some access to education and were thus enabled to push their children into mainstream society. Three generations of my family have worked in the railways and lived in railway quarters. I often wonder where my family would have been, had my grandfather not migrated from his village since, among Dalits, progress is visible mostly in the families of those whose forefathers had secured jobs under British India. Even Dr B.R. Ambedkar, the saviour of Dalits and a man with foresight and intelligence of the highest order, with his relentless struggle could not realize his envisaged integration of Dalits into society. The positive discrimination, affirmative actions and reservations guaranteed in the Constitution of free India have not made much difference to the lives of the majority of Dalit families. We could very easily have been in the same state as impoverished Dalit families living in villages.

Baliah was a semi-literate man. A neighbourhood mosque's priest, Ali Saheb's initiative in educating him paved the way for his sons to receive doctorates and become teachers, and his grandchildren to travel to the countries of their choice to pursue higher education. Baliah foresaw the importance of education and set an example for future generations. He frequently read from the Ramayana and the Mahabharata in spite of his own people asking him not to read the revered texts. It was taboo for a Dalit to read these books, and they were afraid that it would have disastrous consequences. Even fellow Dalits saw it as a validation of their views when he met with a serious accident in which he almost lost his life. But my father was stubborn and stood his ground. In a parallel, his uncompromising stance when it came to obliging his superiors got him into trouble at his workplace and led to him being transferred quite frequently.

My father's world was the railways, where he worked. Punctuality, discipline and the ability to work hard were his strengths. He had no great desire to make his children collectors or bureaucrats; rather, he wanted them to learn good English and become officers in the railways, an institution beyond which he could not see. His environs did not make him think further. He wanted his sons to become stationmasters, like his bosses. And for this, he chose the strongest weapon he knew – education.

Had my father not felt the importance of education, had he not been in the railways, we would probably not have seen the days and good fortune that we did. His determination was responsible for us getting an education despite our poverty and social maladies like segregation and untouchability that were quite prevalent in that era. Apart from doing his regular work, he worked as a coolie to earn some extra money so he could send his children to school. My mother Narsamma also worked in the fields to help raise the money to educate us. My father had not read Ambedkar, but he revolted against the prevailing social system: he knew that only through education could we find emancipation from social evils like untouchability. Denied a formal education himself, he took the greatest care to educate his children. Three of them gained doctorates – a rarity even in families with a history of generations-long education.

I wanted to study deeply the roots of my family. The children of Baliah's grandchildren do not know the history of their family, or the difficulties their past generations faced. This book is an attempt to make them see how inhuman the life of their people has been for generations together. Had I not taken to writing, I would have missed making known our history to later generations of my family in particular, and to Dalits in general, who are these days distancing themselves from their past in their search for better lives. My desire to write this story was strengthened further when I saw a beautiful girl, my own granddaughter, in 2005. She was born in the US. Her rosy lips, curly hair and beautiful round eyes were the most captivating ones I had ever seen. It occurred to me that this child, when she grew up, would probably be alien to India and more so to the Dalit community. She might read American history and about racism and slavery, but what chance would she have to read about the caste system and untouchability, which were more dehumanizing than slavery? Would she ever know where her forefathers came from and whose descendant she was? I started on this book immediately. I worked on it keeping in mind something my father often said, 'Son, whatever work you take up, no matter how small, do it perfectly. Excel in it.' As you would read later, had my great-grandfather not shown excellence in his art of making shoes and presented them to the nizam, our story would have been the same as that of any other Dalit, still suffering indignities.

The contribution of untouchables – often at the cost of their lives – towards the growth of the Indian economy has never been properly recognized or recorded, and they have largely been excluded from sharing the benefits of the resulting economic system.

It is time we started writing our own histories. The stories written by Brahmins beginning with 'Once upon a time, there lived a poor Brahmin ...' should stop now. I feel that it is not my family alone but every Dalit – and non-Dalit – who should know about our past in order to create a better future.

Narsiah's World

A tall man, walking away from his village with a heavy heart, his wife's body tied to his back, and almost dragging a little boy, his son, in a chilly evening drizzle, towards a distant stream that flowed from west to east. It was a small village that he was walking helplessly away from; his three-year-old son weeping aloud as he, half naked, followed his father in the gloomy evening. The village was Vangapalli, in the Karimnagar district of Telangana, the native village of the man. The man with the dead body on his back came from the Harijanwada, the untouchable dwellings in the village. He walked fast so that he could reach the banks of the stream before dark. He was powered by the thought that he had to dig a grave to bury his wife and that he had to do it all by himself. Despite the drizzle, the man was sweating under the weight of his wife's body. Worried whether he would reach the banks of the river by twilight, and cursing his own clansmen who refused to come to his help, he was grieving for his wife, for himself and for the son who had lost his mother.

The man was Narsiah, a Madiga, a chamar (untouchable) by caste, but a man whose father was entitled to fifty acres of agricultural land. An untouchable having such a huge tract of land was unbelievable. But it had been gifted to his father by Nawab Mir Tahaniat Ali Khan Afzal ud Daulah, the nizam of the Deccan. He was the fifth nizam of the

Asif Jahi dynasty, who were the rulers of the area since 1719. Once, when the nizam was passing through this village, Narsiah's father, also called Narsiah, had presented the nizam with a beautiful pair of shoes made from the hide of a young calf. Being of excellent craftsmanship, the shoes were soft as silk and fit the nizam's feet very well. The nizam was fascinated by the shoes; so happy was he that he immediately called his revenue officials and declared a gift of fifty acres of land to Narsiah (senior). It was amazing! A Madiga receiving a huge gift of very fertile land, with two open wells!

This happened during the latter part of the nineteenth century. The structure of the village, though, was almost the same as of today. Most villages in India have for centuries had the same composition. A village has the perfect Hindu caste set-up with all the characteristic features codified by Manu. It has two types of dwellings, varna houses and avarna huts, separated by either a boundary or a well-maintained distance.

In order to avoid pollution (from the casteless untouchables) through wind to caste Hindus, the houses of each varna (caste) are built in such a way that the wind blows from the dwellings of the Brahmins to the rest of the village. Untouchable (avarna) houses are located in the east and the main village in the west, since the wind always blows from west to east. Houses are built in ascending order of the caste hierarchy from east to west – Sudras, Vaishyas, Kshatriyas and Brahmins. The houses of those belonging to the productive caste (the Sudras) cluster together, and towards the east, finally, is the agraharam, Brahmins' dwellings – the 'beginning' of the village.

In the Vangapalli of those days, the Velama caste, a feudal community, was, as today, a powerful group holding vast tracts of land. Although few in number, they were the chiefs of the village, collecting revenue and depositing it into the treasury of the nizam. The word of the chief, the Dora, was law. The Dora knew about every family and each individual in the village, and in this case, he wielded enough power to have access to the young untouchable girls, the most vulnerable group in the village.

The hapless untouchables never dared question the caste Hindus, and suffered every brutality silently. Their condition was such that they were not allowed to walk facing people from the higher castes since even that was considered a means of pollution. Possessing even a small piece of land was a distant dream for these deprived, dispossessed outcasts.

Under such circumstances, Narsiah suddenly found himself owning land, and a lot of it! Could he ever take possession of it? How? He ran to inform his wife, but then halted and stood rooted to the ground for a few seconds when a man called him, saying, 'Arey Narsiga, the Dora is calling you!' He then turned towards the Dora's house, cursing himself for presenting shoes to the nizam. The gift might bring disaster upon him! As he approached him, Narsiah could see the Dora's fury: his face had turned red.

'You son of a bitch, untouchable pig! How dare you present a gift to sarkar and receive land from him?' shouted the Dora.

'Nee gulaponni, Dora, I am your slave. How could I dare do that! I am at your mercy; I live at your feet; forgive me,' said Narsiah, head bent and hands folded, in a low voice. He took care to stand a respectful distance away.

'You bastard, you are an untouchable! What will you do with fifty acres of land? Do you want to become a landlord and start sitting beside me?' roared the Dora.

'No, no, Dora, how can I commit such a sin? An untouchable like me can never become a landlord. God will punish me. I will go blind! You are my lord, Dora!'

The Dora calmed down at this, and looking mercifully at him, said, 'Bastard, take two acres from that gifted land and cultivate it for your family.' Turning to his clerk, he ordered, 'Go and take the rest into account as our land.'

Narsiah felt relieved. He was elated at being allowed to retain the two acres. He was happy that he was saved the wrath of the Dora, happy that the Dora had not had him beaten up.

❋

Narsiah was a respected man in his community. Older than most people, he would settle most disputes within his community. Apart from making footwear, he worked in the fields of the landlord. His wife Pochamma was a gentle lady who worked both at home and in the fields. His son, about fifteen years old, worked as a jeetagadu – a labourer who worked for the landlord day and night without being paid any wage – and often slept in the cattle shed in order to be accessible to the landlord and his family at all times. He was also a confidant of his Dora, and received some grain and paddy when his master felt generous. Narsiah's two daughters were married and lived in the neighbouring village. His family was now better off than most other untouchable families. Although deprived of the vast land gifted by the nizam, he still held two acres, albeit at the mercy of the Dora. Other untouchables had no land at all. Despite being held in high regard by the people of his community, he was humble and friendly.

Narsiah and his wife often argued on the issue of their son's marriage.

'You settle the issues of people in the village, but you have no care about your son's marriage,' Pochamma would say as she ladled cooked broken jowar into his bowl and topped it with mutton curry.

Narsiah, mixing the food in his bowl, would respond slowly, 'I am looking for a good, beautiful girl for our Narsigadu.'

'When? After my death? He is nearly sixteen!'

'Don't shout. I am already on the lookout. Why don't you let me eat my food!' Narsiah would say irritably.

Then she would cool down a little and say, 'Kaadayya, no, dear, don't be angry. It is just that he is past the marriageable age, and people think that we are being irresponsible and letting our son go free.'

'Our son is a good boy. He won't get us a bad name,' Narsiah would say, washing his hands. 'Let me find a beautiful, fair girl for him.'

'I don't know how you will do it, but by the end of this summer my son should be married. Once he is married, the Dora will send him home and he will not have to sleep in the cattle shed, poor boy.' Her worry could be heard in her voice.

It was seven in the evening. After finishing supper, Narsiah left his house, a thatched hut consisting of two rooms that he had recently constructed so that his son could have some privacy after his marriage. The hut was neat and tidy, and it had aluminium kitchenware, raw woollen blankets and even bamboo cots. All this was possible only because he possessed land, which gave him some income. Suddenly, a man came running behind him, 'Arey, Narsiah, where are you? I have been searching for you all day.'

'What's the matter?' Narsiah turned around impatiently.

'You wanted a bride for your son, right? I saw a beautiful girl in the next village.'

Narsiah was very happy. Though he could not see the man's face, he recognized the voice. 'Yelliah! You've given me good news. My wife was taunting me just now. Who is the girl's father?'

'Let's talk at the toddy shop.'

'Oh, no! Yelliah, I've already finished my supper.'

'It's okay, you needn't have a drink if you don't want to, but buy me one. I can't give you such important news for free,' laughed the man, his white teeth shining in the dark. They approached the toddy shop chatting about other things.

As they walked, they saw men and women hurrying towards the toddy shop to retire after working hard through the day. Tapped and sold by men from the Idiga caste, a sub-caste of the Sudras, palm wine was a favourite drink among the villagers. Toddy tappers, also known as gaundlollu, would risk their life and limb to procure toddy from tall palm trees.

Standing in the section reserved for untouchables in the toddy shop, Narsiah yelled out to be served toddy. As the gaundlollu brought the small pot of toddy, Narsiah kept the money at a little distance; the man sprinkled water on the money to remove the pollution of it having been touched by an untouchable before picking it up and turning to serve his other customers. Holding the pot by its rim, Narsiah rushed towards Yelliah.

Sipping the drink, Yelliah said, 'I saw the girl. She is fair and beautiful and must be around ten years old.'

Early marriages were the norm, and at ten, a girl was considered to be of marriageable age. However, after the wedding, she would live with her parents until she reached puberty. There were times when girls became pregnant at the age of twelve or thirteen, leading them to have a tough and dangerous prenatal period. Coupled with this, the lack of hygiene and of sufficient medical knowledge and hospitals meant that deaths of mothers and infants were common. Women would toil till the last minute before delivery. The old women of the community would examine the pregnant bellies to deduce the time of delivery and would assist during the deliveries. They would use sickles to cut the umbilical cord, and collect the placenta in a small earthen pot, which would subsequently be buried. It was customary for people not to ask where one was born, but where one's placenta pot or mayi munta was buried. The situation was the same for caste Hindu women, except that the women assisting during the deliveries would be from the barber caste.

'Who is her father?' asked Narsiah.

'Malliah. You know him well. He lives in the next village. He has three daughters, two of whom are already married. This is the third one.'

'Yes, I know the man. Shall we go tomorrow to see the girl?'

'Yes. We'll start at six in the morning so that we reach by eight.'

Both got up to leave, Narsiah happy and in a hurry to share the news with his wife.

※

It was early in the morning. People in the village were setting about their work. Women walked in groups, with their lunch packs on their heads and sickles in their hands, humming folk songs, towards the paddy fields ready for reaping. Herds of cattle raised dust as young boys prodded them towards the grazing fields with sticks. Narsiah was neatly dressed, a turban on his head, ready and waiting for Yelliah. He wanted to get his son married at the earliest so that the boy could finally spend the nights at home. He hoped that the girl was good-looking; his wife was particular that her daughter-in-law be fair.

'I am sorry, it's late,' Yelliah said as he hurried in.

'It's all right, let's go.'

They walked fast, talking about their village chiefs who treated them and their children worse than animals. From time to time, they looked around guiltily to make sure no one was listening.

It was hot when they reached Malliah's hut. Malliah came out and gave them water to wash their feet. Having exchanged greetings, they sat down on a mat. Yelliah told Malliah the reason for their coming.

'It's very hot,' said Yelliah, removing his turban and wiping his forehead.

'Yes, yes. Would you like some water?' asked Malliah. 'Get some water,' he said to his wife.

The three men exchanged news about people of their community from both villages. Then Malliah went into the next room and asked his wife to get their daughter ready in a new sari.

Narsiah and Yelliah awaited the girl.

'Where is the girl?' asked Yelliah.

'She is shy. Her mother is bringing her,' replied Malliah, smiling.

The girl stood behind the door, peeping at the strangers. She was fair and beautiful. Her mother said with a broad smile, 'I've taught her all household tasks, and she is a fine cook. She is the one who manages the house when we go to the fields.'

'That's good,' said Narsiah, and asked, 'What is her name?'

'She is Abbamma,' replied her mother.

'What does your son do?' asked Malliah.

'He is working at Pedda Dora's. He is fifteen and is as tall as I am,' said Narsiah.

An eager participant in the conversation, Yelliah said, 'He knows every type of work.'

'Is his name Narsiah too?' asked Malliah.

'Yes, it was my father's wish,' smiled Narsiah.

'That's nice. If you agree to this proposal, we shall meet you at your house along with our women,' said Malliah.

'I shall send word to you within a couple of days, after consulting my wife.'

'Shall we have a drink?'

'Not now. We shall drink and celebrate once you come to my house and see my son.'

Very happy on the way back, Narsiah thanked Yelliah for finding him a good match for his son and told him about his willingness to arrange the wedding immediately.

When Narsiah entered his hut, his son was eating his lunch and Pochamma was serving him. Though she was very anxious and curious, she did not mention the subject.

'Would you like to eat?' she asked Narsiah.

'Yes, I am hungry.'

As the son left, he told his mother that he might not return home for the night as he had to drive the Dora's cart the next day and escort him to town.

He looked at his father for permission and left.

'What happened?' Pochamma asked, serving Narsiah food.

'The girl is fair and beautiful,' smiled Narsiah.

'Oh! That is good news.'

'You may also know them. She is Malliah's youngest daughter, Malliah who lives in the neighbouring village.'

'I know them. The family is very good. When shall we fix the marriage?'

'Let's see, I was waiting for your opinion to ask them to come and see our son in a couple of days.'

The girl's parents and close relatives had visited, and they had agreed to the match. They had feasted together. Now Pochamma began preparing for the wedding, inviting her two married daughters to come and help. The house was buzzing with pre-wedding activities. Narsiah's son was, at fifteen, a handsome boy with a good physique, six feet tall and dark-complexioned. The hard work in the fields had made him strong. Being the only son of Narsiah, he had also been given the name Narsiah by his grandfather, and the villagers called him Chinna Narsigadu, or Narsiah Junior. He was well loved by the people in his community, especially the aged, whom he readily helped whenever they needed his assistance.

Narsiah held his son's wedding in the hot summer month of May. A good number of people from both villages gathered to celebrate. The wedding was grand, unlike those held in other families, as Narsiah was well placed among the untouchables. And since he was an elderly, respected person, the people of his community attended in large numbers. Instead of beef, goat's meat was served at the marriage feast. Liquor too was served, and people enjoyed themselves singing folk songs and dancing to the beat of the dappu, a small drum. The wedding would be remembered and talked of by the people of the village for months afterwards.

But soon, the activity and celebratory mood in Narsiah's house subsided; his daughters went back to their houses and the newly wed daughter-in-law returned to her parents' house. Soon it was June, and as the hot weather began to wear itself out, the villagers got busy ploughing the land and readying it for sowing the moment the first rains drenched the fields.

In those days, infectious diseases were widespread in villages, particularly in untouchable dwellings. Cholera was one such disease. Each house had at least a couple of deaths due to cholera. People called this dreadful disease gattara and were even afraid of touching the dead body of a person who had died of the disease. Only the inmates of the house could carry the dead body for cremation.

The deities of the untouchables are goddesses, with different regions having different goddesses. The temples for these deities are very small, usually three or four feet high, with dome-shaped roofs. People offer prayers and such food as they themselves eat to the goddesses. The offerings – made in the hope of the fulfilment of the wishes of the devotees, or when they *are* fulfilled – include toddy and other liquor, and slaughtered goat, lamb or even fowl. The deities they pray to are not the same as the Hindu ones; the Brahmins would contemptuously describe the deities of the untouchables as 'Kshudra Devatas'. Unlike in Brahminism, where the priest is a Brahmin, male and hierarchical, and the Varnashrama Dharma is institutionalized, there are no priests for these deities, and every untouchable is a priest unto himself or herself. Sudras too have these deities in their localities and they worship them in the same way as untouchables do, but the Sudras, besides worshipping these goddesses, also go to Hindu temples. Though placed at the bottom of the caste edifice, they have access to temples since they are still 'touchable'.

In Vangapalli, the disease was attributed to a curse cast upon the village by the angry village goddesses, Mallamma, Yellamma and Katta Mysamma. Superstition was rampant, and it was believed that these goddesses could enter into the bodies of older women, who would then go into a trance.

It was afternoon. Narsiah was sitting under a low awning that he had made of gunny bags, leather chappals strewn all around him. This place was close to his house, but caste Hindus also took this route. He was mending chappals when a man came up running and said, breathing heavily, 'Narsiah! Narsiah! Everyone is looking for you; the goddess has entered Ellamma's body.'

Narsiah dropped his work and followed him hurriedly. They reached a place where a good number of people were standing around the lady in trance; she was swaying about, holding small branches of neem in both her hands. With great reverence, Narsiah bent down and said, 'Mother, we seek your blessings. Be kind to us. Please let us know why you have come.'

'Narsiga, don't you know why I have come? The goddess is very angry, she needs sacrifices, lest the village get gattara,' she said, now swaying violently.

Trembling, Narsiah said in a low voice, 'Shanti, Talli, shanti! Please calm down, Mother. Do you want a large animal or a small one?'

Laughing loudly she said, 'A buffalo, a cartful of rice, toddy and liquor are to be offered to me with a happy heart.'

'Is that all, Mother? We shall definitely offer you all of that.'

'Selvu, selvu, I take leave.' Ellamma fell into the arms of someone standing nearby. As water was sprinkled on her face, she came out of her trance.

Narsiah gathered all the elders of the community in the evening and they decided to celebrate the Mother Goddess's festival the next Friday. People got busy preparing for the festival. Rice and money were collected from each house. Narsiah donated the money to purchase the buffalo and all arrangements were made under his supervision. The houses in the Madiga area wore a festive look. Girls and young women decorated the whitewashed Pochamma temple with neem branches. The threshold of the temple was washed with cow dung, and vermilion and turmeric dots were daubed all over the walls. The buffalo's face was smeared with vermilion and turmeric, and it was brought in a procession by the elders. People beat drums, and some danced to the beats. When it was time, a stout man with a huge chopper slashed the neck of the animal with a single powerful stroke, all the while offering prayers. A cart loaded with cooked rice was brought, and a basketful of this rice was mixed with the buffalo's blood. A basket of vermilion and turmeric powder was placed on the head of an elderly man, and he, along with Narsiah and a few others, walked through the streets, sprinkling the food on the houses. This, they believed, would stop evil spirits from entering the house. In the evening, every house had a good feast, and men and women had a good time drinking toddy and liquor.

Six years passed. There were many changes in the village. Pedda Dora died of a paralytic attack. His son, a middle-aged man, took over the affairs of the gadi, as the landlord's bungalow was called. This consisted of a huge house, a cattle shed, a store for fodder and a closed well. The new Dora was very arrogant, and everyone was afraid of him. The untouchables were terrified to be anywhere within his sight. This Dora summoned Narsiah and demanded that he surrender his two acres of land. When Narsiah did not, his family had to face the Dora's wrath. Besides working for the Dora, Narsiah's son Chinna Narsiah had also started working in their own land. The Dora's henchmen started harassing him; the water supply to their fields was cut. Now they had to depend mainly on rainwater. So they had to stop raising paddy and plant crops that could be grown with rainwater. Chinna Narsiah's young wife Abbamma was often heckled and teased by the Dora's henchmen while she was working in their own land and was, at times, forced to work in the Dora's field. There was a happy addition to the family, though: Chinna Narsiah now had a young son, whom the grandfather named Ramaswamy. The boy was very fair and handsome; he had his mother's complexion and his father's features.

It was a terrible bereavement for Chinna Narsiah when his father died of cholera, followed by his mother, who died a week later. He carried the dead bodies of his parents and buried them with his own hands. After this, things went from bad to worse. Chinna Narsiah no longer held the same importance that he did when his parents were alive and he was left alone with his wife and a young son.

One day, while Narsiah was eating his lunch under the shade of a tree, his wife suddenly said, 'Let us leave this village and go to some other place to live.'

'Yes, I've been thinking the same thing,' Narsiah replied.

They decided that once the harvest was done, they would go to the neighbouring village, where her parents lived.

The village was busy with the harvesting, and the big farmers had already started sending their grains to the towns to sell. The small farmers had to wait for the labourers – the landless Dalits who first worked on the fields of the upper-caste landlords and then on the fields of the upper-caste Sudras with small land holdings – to attend to their fields. The corn in Narsiah's fields was ready to be harvested, and he had requested some women of his community to help him reap the crop. They agreed to do the job in a week's time. There was great pressure on Narsiah to surrender his piece of land to the Dora after the harvesting season. He was very sad that he should be losing his land after his father's death. No one in the village came out in his support since even his clansmen were of the opinion that being an untouchable, he was not supposed to hold land.

One day, Narsiah found his wife shivering with high fever, and vomiting: it was gattara. Narsiah immediately sent word to her parents, who, unfortunately, were not in their village, having gone to visit another of their daughters, who lived in a far-off village. The next afternoon, as her husband and son looked on, Abbamma breathed her last. The end had come suddenly; she was barely sixteen. It was the greatest blow by far for young Narsiah, who wailed like a child and beat his chest. His son lay across the dead body of his mother and wept, but there was nobody to console the father and son. The people of his community had abandoned his house because of the disease. Forsaken and friendless, Narsiah slowly got up and, wiping his tears, drew his son close to himself. He had made up his mind to leave the village.

Narsiah collected his clothes and his son's. A small earthen pot wrapped in cloth hung from the roof; his wife used to save coins in it. The sight caused Narsiah to break down once again. His wife's sudden death made him loath to ask for anything from the villagers. No longer concerned about the crop or the house, he was unwilling to stay there even for a minute. He tried to remember every moment he had spent with her. They had spent very little time with each other. He cursed God for taking his wife away from him so quickly, and for leaving him a young, motherless son. He sobbed as he wrapped his wife's dead body in a cloth. It was drizzling outside as he lifted it gently to his shoulder and tied it to his back. He had a long distance to travel. He wrapped the clothes in a blanket and placed the bundle on the other shoulder. Holding his son's hand, he walked out of the house never to return. Crossing the wada, he looked back with tears rolling down his cheeks, and then picked up his pace as he walked towards the stream.

It was five in the evening and still drizzling when Narsiah reached the stream. He slowly put down his wife's body. Her face seemed fresh; to him, it appeared as if she were looking at him, begging him to take care of her son. He burst into tears again, but composing himself, started digging the grave. Finally, he put his wife to rest. For ever.

It was a premature death; she was like a brilliant meteor that had burnt out as soon as it entered his life. Narsiah hugged his son tight. Both sobbed helplessly for a while. Then he washed his face and little Ramaswamy's in the stream, and offered the child a piece of jowar roti. As the boy ate, he sat, sunk in thought, hugging his knees close. Where was he to go? What was he to do? He was reluctant to go to his in-laws. It suddenly struck him that he should go to his maternal uncles at Jangaon.

He remembered his two uncles well; they would sometimes come to spend a few days with his family, and whenever they came, they brought new clothes, sweets and other eatables for them. They loved him like his mother had loved him, and had often taken him to the toddy shop on their shoulders even when he was just a six-year-old boy. They were sure to take care of him now. With their help, he would be able to find a job and raise his son.

Narsiah determined to go to them. He bathed in the waters of the stream and changed his clothes. Counting the coins his wife had saved, he found that he had four rupees: these would be of great help to him in his long journey. He had more than a hundred miles to go. Placing his son on his shoulders, he began to walk.

It was noon of the next day. Narsiah sat under a shady tree while his son ate a jowar roti. It was one of his breaks during the journey. He lit a chutta – a bit of tobacco rolled by hand into a leaf. The poor man lit it not with match sticks but using two small flat stones with coarse edges, a small, flat, rectangular bit of steel bar and a piece of fine jute fibre. Narsiah thought about what job he could take up in the new place, Raghunathapalli, where his uncles lived. He would reach by evening and he was confident that they would help him secure a job. He had visited his uncles along with his wife in more prosperous times and spent happy days with them. Now he was going to them with his son – it would be very difficult to tell them about the sudden demise of his wife.

Later in the evening, as he approached his elder uncle Malliah's house, the man saw him from a distance and came running to meet him. Lifting up the boy, he asked, 'Where is Abbamma?' Narsiah could no longer control himself. He wailed loudly, covering his face with his palms. A shocked Malliah stood motionless, unable to say anything. The boy in his arms struggled, 'Mother died, father buried her.' Malliah held Narsiah tight, both of them sobbing heavily as the rest of the family gathered around them. The entire Madigawada grew silent with grief as the news spread. Later, sitting in Malliah's hut with his uncles and their families, Narsiah recounted, in a quivering voice, how his wife died and how he had buried her with his own hands. He ended by saying that he had decided to leave his village. His uncles consoled him and said that coming to them was a wise decision. Though she was no more, Narsiah felt that he had come to his mother. Her brothers consoled and comforted him and showered on him the same love and affection that she used to give him. He felt that it was the right place for his son to be, and that he need no longer worry about the child. He was himself no more an orphan. Narsiah finally slept peacefully that night.

It was now three months since Narsiah had moved to Raghunathapalli, but he had not yet found a job. He felt guilty about being dependent on his uncles. He knew that his son Ramaswamy was also being cared for. The child was happy with the other children, but how long could he live off his uncles? Both of them worked as coolies in the railway goods shed. Foodgrains from the nearby villages were packed in big gunny bags and brought in bullock carts to the railway stations. These were shifted into the railway wagons by the coolies, who carried the loads on their backs. This was hard work, done by the untouchables, and for very poor pay. Those like his uncles were better off compared to other untouchables who worked as jeetagallu – men who would work for the landlord but be paid, in kind, when the landlord felt especially beneficent. Even the way the untouchables were addressed, in fact *are* addressed to this day, reflects the deep societal bias against them. A caste Hindu whose name is Malliah remains Malliah, but if he belongs to the untouchable community, he is called Malligadu; the suffix 'iah' is respectable whereas 'gadu' is contemptible. So too among women: the caste Hindu Pochamma becomes Pochi among the untouchables, the venerated 'amma' as distinct from the disreputable 'i'.

Narisah's uncles wanted to find him a job in the railways. When the opportunity presented itself, they appealed to a gora saheb, a British officer who was inspecting their railway station, and requested him to take their nephew into the railways. Narsiah's physique made a good impression on the officer, who ordered him to join as a 'pointsman'. His uncles were jubilant. Narsiah was very happy too, but had one concern – he had to go for a whole month's training. He worried about his son; although he knew that his uncles and aunts would care for him, this was to be the first time he would be parted from his son.

It was the early twentieth century. Except for the princely provinces like Hyderabad, Mysore, and some pockets of Rajasthan and Bengal, the British controlled all of India. To facilitate their own economic growth, they began to take a keen interest in developing the local infrastructure. The technology of the industrialized West was being applied in India for the construction of irrigation systems, including dams and canals, for the introduction and expansion of the railways, the post and telegraph system, and the like. There were too few of the British to manage the Indian administration. So, people from the educated upper castes, mainly Brahmins, were inducted to help run the government at certain levels. Most were trained in London and posted as Indian Civil Service officers in the bureaucracy of the British Indian government. Most of these people were deeply influenced by Western culture and loyal to the British; many tried to adopt the ways of the British even as they worked in the large colonial buildings that came up to house the administrative departments and their various needs. In village administration, though, there was not much change; as earlier, the Brahmins, known as Karnams, were the ones maintaining the land records.

Railroads were laid on a large scale during the late nineteenth century. When the first railway train opened to the public, it was a red-letter day in Indian history: on 16 April 1853 at 3.30 p.m., a train with fourteen carriages carrying 400 passengers steamed out of Bombay station to a twenty-one-gun salute and reached Thane station at 4.30 p.m., covering a stretch of twenty-one miles. This was the beginning of the era of the railways. The Great Indian Peninsula Railway Company, as it was then called, has now turned into the Indian Railways, the world's largest railway network. The British had three excellent reasons for establishing a large railway network: to develop trade and commerce, to establish a quick and efficient administrative network, and to quickly and efficiently quell any threat to their colony from their European neighbours and co-colonizers. Much manual labour was required to lay the railway tracks through the length and breadth of the country, through thick forests and high mountains, and over surging rivers. To such hazardous jobs the untouchables had wide access since, barring a few Sudras, no other 'touchable' was ready to undertake them. People from the untouchable communities were recruited in large numbers all over the country, though even here they constituted the lowest rung. These workers were called gangmen. People in tens used to carry heavy rails on their shoulders through difficult terrain, and accidents were common, sometimes fatal. People also lost their lives to wild animals or poisonous snakes. Nevertheless, the untouchables gained entry into jobs in the railways and into the railway quarters, and started living alongside the Sudras in the same areas, sometimes even the same buildings. The Sudras still tried to maintain untouchability, though. It was a strange situation: untouchables, who were outcasts and segregated in every village, were suddenly living in the same quarters as Sudras! The environment had changed, and now they had the means to learn many new things, not just about work, but about society and social structures too. In many ways, it was the British Indian era that opened the doors of development to the untouchables.

In those early days of the railways, people were also required in large numbers to aid in the formation of trains by coupling coaches to the engines when required, and detaching them when no longer necessary.

This process was known as 'shunting' and those who worked at this job were said to work in the 'operating' department. This department served both passenger and goods trains. A person working thus was at the lowest rung in the job order and was designated as a 'pointsman'. He had a risky job. He had to run between the rails, lift the heavy metal chain (weighing more than 100 kilograms) of a stationary bogie, and couple it with the hook of a bogie approaching slowly from the opposite direction. Although they received training, the hazardous nature of the job frequently cost men their limbs. Pointsmen could get seriously injured if they slipped while running on the tracks; sometimes, they even came under the wheels of the moving bogies. Untouchables came to be recruited throughout India for work in this department.

This was the job that Narsiah had secured. He was posted at a small roadside railway station close to his uncles' village. His job included signalling the arrival and departure of trains by ringing a bell, signalling to fast trains, and walking the long distance to light the kerosene lamps fitted at the outer and home signals. He also had to help the (white) stationmaster's wife in her domestic work. Free from the feudal Dora and away from the village and the people who had turned their backs on him when he lost his parents, he was very happy with the new job. Being a young widower, his uncles were on the lookout for a girl for him.

Ramaswamy was now ten years old. He had been happy in those early days when his father had married again, and his stepmother Ramakka had looked after him well. But that had lasted a very brief period. Now, he had to take care of his five-year-old brother Yelliah and his three-year-old sister Pentamma while their mother was busy; sometimes even when she was not. He had to do all kinds of household jobs and could get rest only when his father was at home. His siblings were preferred over him by his stepmother. He had to wait till his brother and sister ate, and many a time, in the absence of his father, was given only leftovers to eat. Ramakka was envious of the handsome child that Ramaswamy was. She even beat him increasingly frequently, but he bore everything patiently and in silence.

There was a school in the neighbourhood. Ramaswamy was very curious and would always peep into it, particularly when the students were sitting in the classrooms, reading aloud collectively from their books as a teacher sat in a chair at the head of the class. His keen young mind wanted to learn to read and write. But untouchable that he was, he was not allowed to even enter the school. One day, he said to his father, 'Father, I want to go to school.'

Narsiah looked at his son's innocent face, and drawing him close, said, 'Dear child, we are Harijans, they won't teach us.'

'But why?'

'Because we are untouchables.'

'So what? I shall sit far away. I won't touch them in school, just as we don't touch them elsewhere.'

'But the teacher will not teach you.'

'But I won't touch the teacher, either.'

Narsiah had no answer to his son's argument; he was unable to explain to his son the laws of *Manusmriti*, that sage Manu had codified everything about the Hindu way of life, and untouchables had, for centuries together, been segregated. Sin and punishment – papamu and dandana – are infallible tenets of Hindu laws regarding Sudras and untouchables. This ideology conditioned the minds of untouchables to believe that they would be committing a grave sin if they went against this law. According to Manu's laws, touching caste Hindus amounted to a sin, so did standing or sitting in front of them, and wearing a turban or footwear in front of them.

Narsiah could only say, 'No son, we are not supposed to write and read. We commit a sin when we do that'. However, this argument did not satisfy his young son.

After finishing his work at home, Ramaswamy would spend his time watching the school children and their activities from a distance. One day, a mullah who had been observing him for several days came to him and affectionately asked him, 'Do you want to learn writing and reading?'

'But I am untouchable,' the boy replied.

'It does not matter. I will teach you.'

'But how about the sin?'

'Don't worry. I will take care of everything.'

Ramaswamy asked, 'When shall I come to you? I have to finish my work at home before I can come.'

'Come whenever you find time, my child. I am always in that mosque,' he said, pointing to a nearby mosque.

The boy was overwhelmed with joy and told his father. They decided to keep it a secret from his stepmother, lest she stop him from going.

The next day, after finishing his work, he bathed, and having dressed as neatly as he could, he went to the mosque. The mullah was surprised by Ramaswamy's promptness and the interest he showed in learning. He made the boy sit beside him. Ramaswamy, conditioned as he was, moved away slowly, fearing the pollution of his touch! The mullah wrote the first few Telugu letters on a slate and asked the boy to learn by writing over them. Thus it came about that, against all social and religious odds, after many centuries of being denied learning by caste Hindus, a Muslim teacher sowed the seeds of learning in the Yelukati family – something for which the coming generations would be forever indebted to this first teacher of the family.

But things were not going to be easy. Ramaswamy's passion for learning was not encouraged and it lasted only two or three years, until his father was transferred to another station. By that time, though, he could read and write a little, and was always on the lookout for books to practise his skills.

Narsiah knew well enough that his son was not properly looked after by his wife, but he was helpless. His young son never complained; instead, he patiently took care of his siblings, and the children were very affectionate towards each other. But Narsiah was worried because his wife was now forcing him to get Ramaswamy a job. He often overheard his wife taunting his son while he ate. These thoughts troubled him all the time.

Narsiah had been a full-fledged pointsman for a while now, in charge of ensuring that the kerosene signal lamps were maintained and lit as needed. His daily routine did not vary much. One evening, Narsiah was preparing as usual to go to the signals with a bottle of kerosene. Every station had two signal posts on each end: one known as the outer signal and the other the home signal. The pointsman had to go to the outer signal first and then come back to the home signal. The communication system in those days being purely manual, the pointsman had to walk a long distance to pour kerosene into the lamps. The whole process therefore took quite a long time. On this day, when summoned by the stationmaster, Narsiah immediately rushed to the station, leaving behind his lamp and kerosene bottle. He stood ready, awaiting instructions. The stationmaster, clad in a white uniform and wearing a blue cap with an NSR (Nizam-guaranteed State Railway) emblem, was busy sending out a telegram to another station. He did not hear Narsiah come in. Narsiah stood silently listening to the 'kat-gada-gada, kat-gada-gada' of the Morse code as the stationmaster tapped the keys. In those days, the railways used telegraphic language for quick communication; the telephone had not yet been invented.

It was a while before the Anglo-Indian stationmaster looked up and shouted at Narsiah, 'What, man! You came now? I called for you long back.'

'I came in immediately, sir. You were busy sending a message, and I have been waiting for your orders,' Narsiah replied.

'Look, that fellow Malliah is not reporting at zero hours, so you will have to continue. I don't have a substitute.'

'Yes, sir.'

'Did you go to the signals? You have to look at the whole work. The other fellow who was to come has also not reported. The 22 Down passenger is on time. Come quickly after lighting the signals.'

'Yes, sir,' he saluted the stationmaster and left.

Such situations, when Narsiah had to continue working across two shifts, cropped up sometimes. At dusk, it was unsafe for the pointsmen to go to the outer signal. They had to carry a burning torch to protect themselves from wild animals like boars, tigers, etc. Poisonous snakes were an added danger; carelessness could result in death. It was getting darker by the minute today. Narsiah held a torch in one hand and cautiously approached the signal. The tall pole was fitted with a long, rectangular blade at the top; when horizontal, this blade pointed to a red glass circle, signifying 'Stop', and when pulled into an angular position, it pointed to a green glass circle, indicating that the train could proceed. A kerosene lamp was positioned behind the blade in such a way that at night the signal was clearly visible. The blade was manipulated by means of a long cable that ran all the way from a cabin at the railway station to the signal. A system of pulleys made this possible. The cabin man would use a lever to move the blade, and while it only needed two levers in a small station, in big stations and at junctions, there used to be a series of levers in a big cabin. These manual signals have today been replaced by electric lights.

Narsiah lit the signal lamps and rushed back to ring the bell for the incoming passenger train. A small piece of iron rail hanging to a pole was used as the bell, and a big bolt was used to strike it, signalling the arrival of a train. Job done, Narsiah sat on a bench and his thoughts wandered towards his son. Ramaswamy was fourteen now, and he wanted to get him married, but was afraid that his wife might not agree as he did not have a job yet. He would have to find a job for him.

'Narsiah! Where are you? The train is approaching, come in. You need to give a "line clear",' shouted the stationmaster, breaking into his thoughts.

'Yes, sir, coming!' He almost ran.

Every train had to get a 'line clear' before it passed through a station; a metallic tablet imprinted with some letters was released after receipt of a message from the previous station. The pointsman had to hand the tablet over to the engine crew before the train left the station. In case of a non-stop train, the pointsman would use a contraption – a tennis-racket-like device with a long handle to which the tablet was attached in a small pouch, using a thick wire – to deliver the tablet. He had to hold the tablet out by the long handle, standing nearly on the edge of the platform, at a height. The fireman in the speeding engine would grab it by extending his hand and would throw the 'line clear' tablet received from the previous station on the ground. This process required a precise technique and expert handling. Any lapse could make the train stop and the persons involved were liable to a penalty unless they could offer a good explanation. Both the pointsman and the fireman in the engine crew had to remain very alert. At night, the pointsman would hold a flaming torch in the other hand so as to be clearly visible – a sight that never failed to fascinate the children of the railway staff!

It was evening. Narsiah and his colleague Malliah were off duty, and were sitting in a toddy shop.

'You are becoming a stranger to us, trying to even sit alone. What's the matter?' asked Malliah, as he gulped some toddy.

'I am worried about my son, Ramaswamy. He is fourteen now, and I am in a dilemma. Whether to get him married or to find him a job.'

'Oh! Marriage is not a problem; there are many girls around. If you want, I shall start looking for a beautiful girl whom your son can marry.'

'My wife wants him to do a job but he is barely fourteen.'

'That's okay; why don't you try for a job for him in the railways?'

'He is too young for any job here.'

'It does not matter. His physique is good and he is fit, and he looks older than his age. It would be better that he take a job. Franklin Sir is coming to our station next month for inspection. You could ask him then.'

'Is that so? I will surely try.'

Franklin Sir was the assistant personnel officer, a white officer overlooking a number of stations, and with the authority to appoint people to jobs, and remove them if they did not perform.

Both finished their drinks and got up.

Narsiah had now decided that he would get Ramaswmay a job before thinking about his marriage.

※

Ramaswamy was up late, waiting for his father for dinner.

'Son, you could have finished your dinner. Why did you wait for me?' he asked his son as he washed his feet.

'I feel happy eating with you at least once a day.'

'Oh! My son, I love you as much as I loved your mother; but see how you have grown up! It is time for you to even get a job.' Narsiah became emotional, his eyes damp with tears.

Ramaswamy was smiling, though, as he served him jowar roti and mutton curry.

'It's fine, Father, one has to work when one grows up. I shall work, don't worry.'

Father and son fell silent, both having more to say than they could readily utter.

Narsiah broke the silence. 'Son, next month, Franklin Sir, our officer, is coming here. I will request him to offer you a job. He is a good man.'

'That's good of you, Father. I shall do any job,' Ramaswamy was pleased. 'Mother will be happy.'

'Yes, Son, I am worried about your mother taunting you all the time.'

'Oh, Father, don't worry, I'm fine.'

They finished their meal. Narsiah was happy that he was able to talk freely to his son while his wife was asleep. His only worry now was that his son was too young to work, but he could be happy and peaceful once he had a job. His second son, Yelliah, encouraged by his elder brother, was also getting an informal education. The stationmaster was teaching him English in the evenings at his residence. The stationmaster's wife didn't like it and so the child was made to sit outside the house. This humiliation, as we call it now, never affected the young child since he took this segregation to be a way of life.

In those days, electricity had reached only the big cities and a few commercial centres. The railway stations were mostly dark, except here and there where a kerosene lamp flickered. In small stations, only in the stationmaster's office would there be a little light from a big kerosene lamp.

Winter had set in and a cold wind was blowing. It was around nine or ten in the night, and the platform was shrouded in darkness except for a bleak light in the stationmaster's room. Nothing was visible. Narsiah and two of his colleagues sat wrapped in thick raw blankets (supplied to the ground staff by the railways) around a fire, smoking.

'When is Franklin Sir coming for inspection?' asked Narsiah, rubbing his palms and warming them by the fire.

'Sometime soon,' replied one of the men sitting next to him.

'How do you know that?'

'The other day I heard the stationmaster saying that he was going to install a pankha soon and that he was also making arrangements for whitewashing the station.'

A pankha was a manual fan, a large thick cloth, three to four feet wide and almost as long as a room. It was draped over a long wooden rod that hung from the ceiling. A thick rope hung from the centre. A person would swing the cloth using the rope, thus making the air circulate and cooling the room. In smaller stations, this too was part of the duties of pointsmen.

'Is that true?' It was a pleasant surprise to Narsiah.

'Yes, I am sure. I heard it from the stationmaster.'

The stationmaster called, and the other man got up and hurried into the stationmaster's room.

'How long is your son going to sit at home?' shouted Ramakka. 'He has grown up. I cannot feed him any more.'

This was one of Ramakka's constant grievances against Ramaswamy. The family, unlike other untouchable families, actually lived a comfortable life, though not in luxury. There was no struggle for food, shelter and clothing as the wages from the railways took care of these necessities. This was the case with most untouchable families working in the railways. They could even think of educating their children. For these very reasons, these families were also alienated from their own communities in the villages.

'Don't worry. My son is going to get a job,' Narsiah responded, trying to keep his cool.

'You have been telling me that for a year now.'

'He is too young to work.'

'Yes, it appears so to you. Do you know, the boy next door is already working in the fields and helping his mother?'

'So what? I won't send my son to work in the fields.'

'Then what do you want him to do?' she began shouting again. 'Is he a ladsahib?'

'My son is not illiterate. He will not work in the fields. I will find him a good job in the railways,' he said, confidently.

'Hell! Do it soon, then. I am fed up with seeing him at home.'

'Okay, okay. Stop the taunts. He will get a job soon.'

Ramaswamy was quietly listening to the whole exchange, and was determined to work. He did not like to see his father trying helplessly to defend him. He was never troubled when his stepmother hurt him, but felt hurt when she spoke harshly to his father. As his father was about to leave for the station, he said in a low voice, almost whispering, 'Ayya, I will go to the fields.'

'No son, you are no burden to me. Franklin Sir is coming in a few days. I shall beg him to give you a good job,' he said, drawing his son close to him and caressing him affectionately, while his other children looked on, smiling. The other children were also unhappy with their mother's behaviour towards their father and brother. In fact, Narsiah's sons were very affectionate towards each other, and the two pampered their younger sister Pentamma. Even at eight, she was very beautiful: fair, with large eyes, a straight nose, and thick, long, black hair. People often commented that she looked like a velama (upper caste) girl.

The next day, the station was very busy and wore a new look. Everyone from the staff was present, every face was tense. The stationmaster, the assistant stationmaster, and all the pointsmen and gangmen were present in crisp uniforms. It was absolutely neat and tidy, and every record in the stationmaster's room was in perfect order. The stationmaster was giving instructions to each member of the staff. He instructed a pointsman to give a loop line signal to an incoming goods train since the main line was kept ready for the train bringing in the inspection team. The staff members whispered among themselves, 'When will Franklin Sir arrive?' As the much-awaited train steamed into the platform, the stationmaster, clad in a spotless white uniform and a blue cap with the railway emblem, ran towards the coach to receive Mr Franklin, an officer in his early twenties. All the personnel had taken their respective positions, the whole performance having been rehearsed earlier. Mr Franklin was pleased with both the look and the work of the people working at the station; he even complimented the stationmaster and his staff for their efficiency. After lunch, he sat in a big armchair, resting, while a pointsman pulled the pankha. Now everyone, including the stationmaster, was waiting for the train by which the officer would leave.

Narsiah had spoken to Mr Franklin about a job for his son, and was happy that the officer had instructed the stationmaster to remind him about it when he reached Secunderabad. His son, standing by his side, was also happy. Narsiah was anxious to convey the good news to his wife.

In the evening, it was a pleasant surprise for Narsiah to find his uncle Yelliah at home, chatting with his wife.

'When did you come, Uncle? Hope everything is well,' he said, as Ramaswamy ran to hug Yelliah.

'I've just arrived. Everything's fine,' he said, smiling as he looked at his grandson.

'Uncle, you have come at the right time. There's good news.'

'What news?'

'Your grandson is getting a job in the railways. The officer has promised him a job.'

'Oh, really! That *is* good news!' said Yelliah, happy and musing that it had been a wise decision for his late sister's son to come over to them when he lost his wife.

Narsiah hurried out to get toddy for his uncle while his wife prepared a meal for them. It was a special meal. After eating, Yelliah and Narsiah sat outside, smoking.

'Uncle, I have to find a girl for Ramaswamy and would like to get him married before he takes up the job.'

'Yes, I came today for that very purpose.'

'What!' Narsiah said, surprised, 'and you did not mention that until now!'

'I thought I should talk to you first.'

'Oh! Have you seen the girl?' Narsiah was very anxious.

'Yes, she is Karpati Malliah's eldest daughter. She is about ten years old, and they live in Bibinagar. He is a gangman. I have sent word to him that we are coming to see the girl next week.'

'That is good.'

'I shall also speak to your wife tomorrow morning before heading home by the afternoon train.'

Tired by now, the two men went to bed.

Karpati Malliah worked at the Bibinagar railway station, about forty kilometres from Secunderabad. He had migrated from Turkapalli, a nearby village. He had three daughters, Narsamma, Sayamma and Laxmamma, and a foster-son, Ramiah. The oldest of these children was ten. People called Malliah stingy since he did not help anyone, taking care only of his own family. He had put up a big shed behind his quarters, in which he reared goats: he had more than a dozen of them. His son would take them into the open rocky areas nearby and the goats would graze amidst the bushes and shrubs the whole day. Malliah supplemented his income by selling milk and old goats, and was therefore richer than most untouchables. He was a self-made man, and respected in his community for he was a reasonably rich man. His wife, a gentle lady, had died during the birth of their third child. Despite pressure from his kinsmen, Malliah did not marry again since he feared that his children might be subjected to stepmotherly treatment. In untouchable families, it was common for girls to learn every kind of work at home and to even accompany their mothers to work in the fields by the age of eight or nine. Malliah, though, never sent his children to work in the fields. He was now looking for a boy employed in the railways for his first daughter, Narsamma.

Narsamma had an attractive personality. A healthy girl, she was neither fair in complexion nor dark; neither tall nor short. Her eyes were large, and her nose a little snub, but there was a glow on her face. She was very patient, looked after her siblings, and was a great help to Malliah. She could cook all the staple dishes of Madiga families. Malliah saw his wife's image in her and loved her greatly. He was sad at the thought of her marriage, since she would then be parted from him. He had got jewellery made especially for her: silver anklets, hollow armlets of silver, and a nose stud or chinna puste. Puste is a pair of small discs of gold, one larger than the other. The smaller of the two is called chinna puste and is made especially for a girl's wedding by her parents. The larger one, known as pedda puste, is bought by the groom's parents. These are threaded to a cord soaked and dried in turmeric paste, and this cord is tied around the bride's neck by the bridegroom, uniting the couple in marriage. The fact that the chinna puste was waiting in readiness for Narsamma made both the children and the elders around her tease her about getting a husband soon.

When Malliah received Yelliah's message that he was bringing Narsiah and his wife over to see the girl, he busied himself at once. His sister, who lived in a nearby village, came to help with the preparations. She guided the girls about the house, and helped Narsamma get ready. Malliah went to the station to receive the visitors, waiting there since the train was late by an hour. When Yelliah arrived with Narsiah and his wife, he received them warmly, and in a few minutes they were all at Malliah's quarters.

Narsamma was very tense, and sat silently as the strangers watched her. She was shy, and held the corner of her sari close to herself. Narsiah's wife nodded her head approvingly. Yelliah and Narsiah were happy. They had toddy but refused food since they were doubtful whether it was auspicious to eat at Malliah's house like relatives before the wedding was formally fixed.

Back home, Narsiah sent word to Malliah that they were agreeable to the alliance and invited him to his house to see his son. He was happy that his son's wedding, his beloved Abbamma's son's wedding, would now take place shortly. Although Narsiah had spent a very short period with his first wife, it had been the best part of his life and a memorable time. Narsiah was shaken out of his thoughts by the stationmaster.

'Hey man, Narsiah, there's some good news for you.'

'What news, sir?' Narsiah was excited. 'Is it regarding my son's appointment?'

'No, man, it is your transfer order.'

'Where to, sir?' He was suddenly worried about a potential displacement.

'Don't worry, man. It is to Secunderabad.'

A large station. That was good. But even so ...

'Sir, what about my son's ...' he murmured.

'Oh! I forgot to tell you, Franklin Sir had sent a message. Your son will get orders soon.'

Narsiah was now doubly happy. It was going to be a privilege to work in such a big station. This, he felt, was a very good omen – Narsamma, the girl they had gone to see, had brought good luck already. She would be good for his son. The master told him that he would be relieved soon, in the next couple of days, and would be sent to Laskar (Arabic for 'cantonment') as Secunderabad was colloquially known. In those days, the twin cities of Secunderabad and Hyderabad were called 'Laskar' and 'Patnam' (Telugu for 'city'), respectively. His joy knew no bounds; he felt that he had achieved everything he wanted. After receiving the transfer orders, he returned home immediately and informed his wife and children that they must pack and prepare to set out for Secunderabad in two days. Ramakka, no less than the children, was excited about the relocation to a big city.

Secunderabad, built in 1804 and named after Sikander Jah, Asaf Jah III, was mostly meant as an accommodation for thousands of military personnel. After signing a treaty with the nizam in 1798, Col Lang established this city as the headquarters of the British subsidiary force. By 1806, Secunderabad was the largest British cantonment in India. The names operational back then, such as Regimental Bazaar, Rifle Range, Bolaram, Bolaram Bazaar and Cavalry Barracks, are still in use today, and most are still cantonment areas. There has been a cultural difference in the people living in Hyderabad and Secunderabad. In Hyderabad, Muslims and Hindus live together in an amalgamation of culture whereas in Secunderabad there's a beautiful blend of Hindu and Christian ways of life. The city's unique culture means that there is a marked difference in the way of life of the general population of Secunderabad and the people living in its railway quarters. Secunderabad was free from communal tensions and many Anglo-Indians lived in the railway quarters too. Today, though, their numbers have dwindled.

The Secunderabad station was, and remains, one of the largest railway stations in the country. Built in 1874 under the Nizam-guaranteed State Railway, the station is built in the style of the Asif Jahi school of architecture. The original large fortress-like structure still stands, although now large annexes flank either side of the building, making it a very large station. The station has several platforms and over 30,000 passengers use it daily. Secunderabad, connected as it is to all the important cities across the country, is an important link between north and south India. It retains its architectural identity despite several metamorphoses over time: new railway yards, additional platforms, modern cabins, electric tracks, etc.

It was in the late 1930s that Narsiah and his family moved to Secunderabad. It was a move that changed everything not only for Narsiah, who was for the first time exposed to a big city, and found himself very busy throughout his eight working hours, but also for his family. Laskar is significant indeed in the lives of the Yelukatis; three generations of the family have served in the railways while based there, and the children of two have spent their childhood there. They have been witnesses to the transformations that have taken place over time:

from manual signals to electric and electronic signals, from telegraphic messages to communication via computer, from howling steam engines to silent, high-speed electric engines. Correspondingly, there have been changes in the Yelukati family.

※

Malliah visited Narsiah in Secunderabad. Narsiah was very happy with his son, who was to take up duty as a 'box man' at the Bellampalli railway station shortly. Ramaswamy, going on fifteen, was a strong lad with a good physique. He underwent the requisite medical tests and received a fitness certificate that qualified him to join the railways. His father took all possible care to provide whatever else was required. His stepmother was somewhat unhappy since she was losing a source of ready help at home, but it was his siblings who stood to miss him the most: they were going to lose both a playmate and a helpmate. Narsiah, though sad at the thought of Ramaswamy's departure, was also happy that he was going to build a life of his own, and even more, that he would be away from his stepmother. On his part, Ramaswamy was ready, excited at the prospect of work; he would repeatedly check his trunk to see that nothing was missing.

'Be careful, my son. Go and see my friend; stay with him until you get accommodation,' Narsiah's eyes were damp, his voice feeble.

'Ayya, don't worry about me, I shall do as you say.'

Ramaswamy's eyes were brimming with tears too. Father and son had hardly stayed away from each other before. Ramaswamy also wiped away the tears from the cheeks of his young brother and sister; it was difficult for him to leave them, but it was time to live on his own. He picked up his trunk and left for the station with his father.

The train was moving; Ramaswamy stood at the door of the coach, waving farewell to his father who stood on the platform. After the train had pulled away, Narsiah simply sat squatting on the platform for a few minutes. He was trying to console himself that he should not worry any more about his son, who was now going to have a life of his own.

Ramaswamy was inducted into the railways at Bellampalli, a moderately big station which supplied water and coal to the rail engines, and was a transit point for goods trains. As a box man, Ramaswamy had to carry the big wooden trunks provided to the guards by the railways. Since it took two or three days for each journey, the guards had to carry not only their clothes and other essentials, but also rations with them. Ramaswamy had to go to the guards' quarters, collect the trunks and place them in the guards' van at the tail end of the train.

At Bellampalli, Ramaswamy enjoyed an independent life, but he missed his father sorely. When there was nothing to do, he would be found in a corner of the railway platform, reading, and people found it very surprising to see an untouchable reading a book. He could write letters to his father – it was amazing; education had somehow trickled down to an untouchable boy in the 1930s to the extent that he could experience the wonder of learning all by himself. He was discouraged and sometimes even condemned by people of his own community, who told him that it was a sin for untouchables to read and write. But the boy never yielded to this pressure and instead often hid himself from public view while reading. It was this tenacity that in later days fuelled his determination to have his own children educated. Though an untouchable, Ramaswamy was liked by all caste Hindus for his behaviour and punctuality at work. He soon became popular even among the wives of the guards, whom he helped when they needed some work done outdoors.

Bellampalli is an important commercial station: extensive coal mines are to be found within an area of about 500 square kilometres along the nearby Godavari River valley, covering three districts of Telangana – Khammam, Karimnagar and Adilabad. Large amounts of coal are transported from here to meet the industrial requirements of several parts of the country. Bellampalli has a vast railway yard to accommodate goods trains and coal vans.

Ramaswamy had lived on his own for a month, and was eager to meet his father to hand over his salary, the first earnings of his life. He was very happy that he could now support his father, and that his stepmother could no longer taunt or humiliate him. The thought that he could now materially help his brother and sister made him happier still. He sought leave for two days to go to Secunderabad. Meanwhile, his father had also written requesting his presence at home.

Narsiah was very proud of his son, who was the only person in the untouchable community who could read and write. When he received a letter, he would show it to his colleagues, each one of whom, like him, was illiterate. A yardmaster at Secunderabad read the letters out to him. One day, Narsiah was pleasantly surprised to see Ramaswamy at the door. He hugged his son, 'How are you, my son? I would have come to the station.'

'I'm fine, Father,' Ramaswamy smiled. Behind Narsiah, he could see his brother and sister coming joyfully to meet him.

'Isn't Mother here?'

'She will be back soon. She has gone to the monad, the vegetable market to get vegetables,' Narsiah smiled. 'She has had to take over those duties now!'

Ramaswamy looked on proudly as Yelliah and Pentamma eagerly examined his bags and exclaimed excitedly as they discovered the new clothes that he had brought for them. Narsiah noticed that his son had lost a little weight and that his fair skin was now tanned. But he was happy for his son.

Ramakka came in even as they spoke about her. Ramaswamy, who had never lived away from his family before, was very happy to see her.

He immediately pulled out all the money he had left from his salary and handed it to her. She smiled at him, 'Give it to your father.'

Ramaswamy said, 'No, Mother, it is for you.'

Narsiah was happy with his son's spontaneous gesture and felt proud that his son had also educated himself in the real sense. Whenever he read, which was often, it was like a dream for Narsiah. He could not take his eyes off the boy at such times.

That night, they were all sitting in the veranda of their tiny quarters (which usually consisted of a room, a kitchen and a veranda) when Narsiah took the opportunity to talk to his son about his wedding.

'Son, it is time for you to get married. I've found a girl for you.'

'Ayya, let me work for at least a year.'

'No, Son, you are nearly sixteen, and are growing older.'

'I need a daughter-in-law to help me,' his mother said firmly.

'Your mother is right, Son,' said Narsiah.

Ramaswamy accepted their decision and said no more. Father and son talked late into the night – the son narrating his experiences, the father listening and sometimes sharing his own.

Malliah was anxious to get his daughter married at the earliest; he had two more daughters who were to reach marriageable age soon. He sent a message to Narsiah to fix a date and discuss the matter in detail. Narsiah, having decided that his son should get married, went with his wife to meet Malliah when he had a day off.

'How is your son?' asked Malliah, offering water.

'He's fine.' Narsiah smiled, 'Is your daughter not here?'

'She is inside.'

'What would you propose to offer the boy in marriage?' asked Narsiah's wife in a low voice, hesitant to discuss the issue.

'We will offer everything that others in the community offer,' replied Malliah.

'It is all right,' intervened Narsiah, and brought the discussion to a close.

They had a feast at Malliah's. He served liquor, and the food cooked by Narsamma was delicious. Eating goat meat and rice was a luxury in untouchable families, and that was what Malliah had arranged for. They fixed the date of the wedding.

Ramaswamy was back at work. The news of his engagement had spread, and everyone was happy for him. Occasionally he would go with his friends to the toddy shop. However, much of his time was spent reading. It was just a beginning, this entry of untouchables into a cadre of government service where education was not a required condition. However, it put the Sudras and the untouchables in close proximity. As yet, untouchability was strictly observed, particularly by women. Ramaswamy, unlike his Sudra colleagues, was not allowed to enter the houses of the upper-caste guards. He often had to wait outside till the guard's trunk was brought out by the man's wife – many wives cursing the untouchable box boys. The women insisted that their husbands sprinkle water on the box once it was placed in the railway van, and they did the same when it was brought to the house. The practice didn't seem strange to Ramaswamy; he was used to it. The Sudra and untouchable women who lived adjacent to each other frequently quarrelled in the yard in front of their quarters. Any object touched involuntarily by an untouchable woman could cause a quarrel. It happened so often that the men began to ignore it. Manu's Varnashrama Dharma was developing cracks.

'Narsamma, are you coming? The engine is here.'

'Yes, coming,' shouted Narsamma, rushing out of her house holding a huge brass pot.

Water in many places in India, like in Bibinagar, has high fluorine content and is not suitable for drinking. The steam engines of those days carried large quantities of water, and at the smaller stations, the women living in the railway quarters would rush to the railway engines whenever they stopped, so they could collect the water that the drivers released through a pipe connected to the water tank. Women, jostling each other, gathered to collect the water. If an untouchable woman touched a caste Hindu woman while filling water in this melee, the latter would throw away the water while also casting the choicest abuses at the other.

Narsamma and her friend were walking back to their quarters with their brass pots on their heads, wiping away the water spilling from their full pots, when her friend asked, 'Are you getting married?'

'Yes, I will go to Laskar,' she replied.

'Oh!' The friend was suitably impressed. 'Laskar is a big city. Have you seen it before?'

'No.'

'Does your fiancé live in Laskar?'

'No, his parents live there,' she said, and shyly added, 'He works at Bellampalli.'

The conversation ended abruptly as the girls parted, each heading towards her house.

Malliah was busy making arrangements for his daughter's wedding. His sister had come to help. Narsiah and his wife were visiting that evening, and he wanted to treat them to a feast. He sent his son to get fresh toddy from the toddy tapper, while Narsamma helped her aunt cook lamb curry and rice.

As soon as she saw the visitors, Narsamma tried to hide herself. As they washed their feet and entered the house, she pressed herself shyly against the wall, and crept out of the other door. As Malliah exchanged pleasantries and offered them seats, Ramiah brought in a pot of still frothing toddy and placed it in front of them. Drinking, they began to discuss the arrangements.

'Bawa, it was my late wife's desire that the wedding be held at our house,' Malliah finally said, having taken a long time to bring it up.

'I thought we could have it at my place, but if it is my sister's desire, I quite accept,' Narsiah smiled.

Malliah was relieved. He said happily, 'Bawa, the wedding will be a grand affair. I won't skimp on expenses.'

His boast was owing to the effect of the toddy rather than confidence, and Narsiah recognized this. He did not drink as much himself; after all, he had to go home that evening.

Narsamma's younger sister Laxmamma brought in the food, and they ate to their hearts' content. The visitors left soon after.

Narsiah was glad since he felt that the girl he had chosen for his son would make him happy. She was beautiful and had attractive eyes. Moreover, she was good at housework and cooking. He remembered Abbamma: his son looked so much like her. He had left his village to save his son, that precious gift of hers, from becoming a jeetagadu. He was happy to be thus liberated from slavery under feudal lords. That migration had changed the course, not only of his own life, but also of the generations to come. He felt this intensely since he perceived the change in the atmosphere and in the new lifestyle that they had since come to adopt in the city. He was even happier for his son, who had become literate. He could never have foreseen this, but he knew now that subsequent generations would also receive an education. He must ask Ramaswamy to ask for an extended leave. The wedding was scheduled for May ... Narsiah's daydream came to an abrupt halt as the train reached Secunderabad.

Just a few days were left for the wedding. Malliah was busy with the arrangements. Among the untouchables, an elderly person known as baindlaina performs the wedding ceremony. Malliah had arranged for a good baindlaina and had carefully chosen four tender goats for the feast. He had arranged for the Idigas to supply enough toddy for all the guests. His quarters had been whitewashed, its roof covered with palm leaves, and a shed-like structure with a cloth roof, a pandal decorated with mango leaves had been erected in the yard. A small earthen pot painted in the ritual colours of white and red, with turmeric and vermilion dots, was filled with rice and tied to one of the poles in front of the house, with an oil lamp placed on it. This was to be lit every night until the wedding was over. The bride-to-be was supposed to stay at home for seven days before the ceremony. She would, in these days, be given a special bath every morning and evening. Over these days, at least five different muttadulus (married women whose husbands are still alive) would smear turmeric paste on her body, singing folk songs, before she was bathed, and she would wear a new sari after each bath and eat rich food. This ritual, known as pendli pillan cheyyadam (the making of a bride), would render the girl 'fit' for marriage. Every day, a close relative of the bride would carry out this ritual of 'bride-making'. In the course of the week, Narsamma put on a little weight, her skin began to glow and she looked more beautiful than ever.

The day before the wedding, it was customary to have a visitor from the groom's side, and Malliah waited expectantly. Soon he saw Yelliah, Narsiah's uncle, coming along briskly, holding something covered in a white cloth. Yelliah smiled at Malliah as he washed his feet. Sitting down, he said, 'The train was late. I was worried that I wouldn't get here before dusk.'

'Yes, I was wondering, too,' Malliah replied.

Yelliah had brought a packet containing turmeric paste for Malliah. As per the custom, a portion of the turmeric paste applied on the groom was to be applied on the bride. Malliah sent it in. Yelliah now took out another packet, this one containing two Haali (nizam's currency) rupees wrapped in white cloth.

'My nephew sent holy paisalu.'

It was a practice among the Dalit and Sudra communities, particularly in the Telangana region, for parents of the groom to send some money to the bride the day before the wedding.

'Oh! It is alright,' said Malliah, taking the packet.

Yelliah was served good drink and excellent food before he left.

The next day was important: the Yelukati and Karpati families were to be united. It was to be the day that led to the history that is about to be related.

It was about ten in the morning. The Bibinagar railway station was full of people waiting to receive the marriage party. The train finally steamed in and Narsiah got out, along with Ramaswamy and others. Ramaswamy was clad in a white dhoti and shirt, both of which had almost turned yellow because of the turmeric and vermilion powder sprinkled on him. A basingam – a crown cut out of thick cardboard and pasted over with glazed coloured paper, decorated with coloured stones and artificial pearls – was tied to his forehead. From his shoulder hung a heavy packet of rice wrapped in a white cloth. The party was welcomed by Malliah and his relatives. Somebody adjusted Ramaswamy's basingam, and then he was led in a procession towards Malliah's quarters. Some children danced in front of the procession, and Malliah, who was leading it, looked about proudly. It was probably the first time that the upper castes had seen a wedding procession of untouchables almost as grand as their own.

The procession stopped at the entrance of the pandal. Some women from the party now stepped forward: they were muttadulus and carried gifts for the bride in big brass plates. Two older women from the bride's party came forward to receive the plates from them. First, though, they washed the women's feet ceremonially with water mixed with vermilion and turmeric. Cooked rice mixed with turmeric and vermilion was thrown on the people from whom the plates were received to ward off evil spirits before the plates were taken from their shoulders. After this, everyone entered the pandal.

Using rice, the baindlaina had made a large rectangle on the ground. A small circle was drawn at each corner of this rectangle, and in each circle, earthen pots were placed one on top of the other, with the smallest on top. These pots had been whitened with lime, decorated with yellow, and interconnected with a series of threads. A yoke, on which the bride and bridegroom sat during the ritual, was placed inside the rectangle. Small drums beat continuously, loud and rhythmic, as Ramaswamy was lifted bodily by his brother-in-law Ramiah and brought into the pandal, and gently made to sit for the ceremony.

Narsamma's aunt had helped her dress. She looked beautiful in her attire: a sari, and jewellery made of silver – anklets, armlets and kamarbandh. She was wearing earrings and a ring made of gold. The baindlaina asked her to sit on the yoke. She was ushered into the pandal by her aunt and others of her family. Not used to the heavy and elaborate clothing, she walked with slow steps.

The drums kept up their beat. Malliah and Narsiah were meanwhile busy receiving guests. Unlike the Brahmin priests, the baindlaina rendered just one Sanskrit shloka 'Shuklambara dharam ...' to solemnize the wedding. Finally, on the instructions of the baindlaina, Ramaswamy tied the puste around Narsamma's neck, while the drums reached a crescendo. After the wedding, goat meat and rice were served to the guests, along with plentiful toddy. Malliah was complimented on the excellent arrangements. The wedding had been lavish by the community's standards. This had been possible only because it was in the railway quarters and not in a village, where higher-caste landlords would never have allowed such pomp and show by the untouchables.

Now it was time for Narsamma to bid farewell to her family and leave the place she had always known as home. The thought of his daughter leaving him was unbearable for Malliah and his eyes filled with tears.

Narsiah's wife and a few others had counted the brass bowls and brass pots that Malliah had gifted, and packed them in a sack. Narsamma's aunt had packed her clothes in a small trunk. Just then, someone came along to inform them that the train had already left Bhongir. On hearing this, everyone made haste to leave for the railway station.

Narsamma washed the wooden threshold of her house, and applied turmeric and vermilion dots on it – an important ritual of farewell when the bride leaves her paternal home. Narsamma's eyes were red with weeping. Malliah took her hand and put it in Narsiah's, choking as he said, 'Bawa, she's a motherless child, look after her well.'

'Bawa, don't worry, she is my daughter now,' Narsiah said, his eyes brimming with tears too.

Ramaswamy was too young to say anything to his father-in-law, but felt the pain of separation that the father and the daughter must be enduring.

Having boarded the train, Narsamma felt a little better. She was travelling in a train for the first time in her life, and was amused to see that the trees and other stationary objects appeared to move. Her aunt, who was accompanying her, was happy that her mind had been diverted. Ramaswamy kept trying to draw her attention by talking loudly, and was thrilled when she looked at him through the corners of her large eyes and smiled. As they approached Secunderabad, the sight of the big buildings surprised Narsamma. She had never seen such buildings before. Nor had she seen more than one train moving at the same time! It was a new experience for her to walk on a big platform, and newer still when they had to cross an enormous railway yard. Narsamma tightly held on to her aunt's hand, constantly looking around, perhaps a little afraid. Her heart beat fast: she was in a land that was very unfamiliar to her.

They reached the small quarters at Bhoiguda. Narsamma and her aunt stood at the door while an elderly woman brought a pitcher of water which had been coloured with turmeric and vermilion. Holding the pitcher high over Narsamma, the woman circled it thrice around her and sprinkled the water on either side. This ritual was to ward off any evil spirits that might have followed the newlyweds. Then, washing Narsamma's face with a little water, the woman asked her to enter her new home, stepping in with her right foot first.

The goings-on made Narsiah remember the time he had spent with his first wife. How restlessly he had waited for her to get him a pack of food in the afternoons! He remembered her carrying the pack on her head and smiling broadly at him. She would serve him and cajole him to eat, not letting him leave even a speck uneaten. Sometimes she brought him roasted peanuts. Narsiah came out of his reverie smiling to himself.

It was evening and the relatives had begun to leave. Neighbours dropped in, curious to see the new bride, and whispering among themselves – the bride was not as fair as the bridegroom; she was beautiful, though. Narsamma's aunt insisted that she keep her head down. She was not to speak to her husband in the presence of the elders; she was learning how to live with her in-laws. Yelliah and Pentamma tried to stay close to Narsamma, to whom everything was new and strange. Her life had been changed completely in the space of a few hours. She had left behind all her people and come to live with a new family. She had changed from Karpati Narsamma to Yelukati Narsamma. A young ten-year-old who had had no worries till the day before had today entered a life of considerable responsibility. Her aunt's presence gave her strength; she knew she would guide her. At the end of the day, tired, she slept with her aunt in a corner of the room.

There came a change in Ramaswamy's lifestyle: no more did he have to wash his clothes himself, or even wash his dishes after a meal. His wife took care of it all. A week soon passed, and it was time for him to return to Bellampalli. He had made many attempts to talk to Narsamma, both directly and indirectly through his brother and sister, but she always ran away smiling. It was not possible for them to sit and talk in his father's small house; moreover, Narsamma was too shy to respond. And now it was too late. He was leaving by the evening train. He saw her folding his clothes and putting them in a bag.

His father told him, 'Ayya, you should apply for quarters. Request the stationmaster for one. Tell him that you will be bringing your wife.'

'Yes, father, I shall ask him.'

Ramaswamy was looking forward to his wife joining him. When he took the bag from her, she did not look at him. She looked down instead, a little crease of worry on her face. When her husband was about to leave, she finally looked at him from behind the door, a weak smile on her face.

The new bride was not allowed to do any work for a while. Malliah had raised her with great care, and except fetching water, he had not let her do any household work. But now she had to get up early and sweep the floor, clean the dishes, wash clothes and do all kinds of work through the day. She walked to and from the well, lifting the heavy brass pot several times a day. Twice a week, she had to ground jowar into flour using grinding stones.

Sometimes, Narsamma had to pound chillies into a paste in a mortar, and this led to burning palms. For a girl her age, it was a strenuous job. Her palms filled with sores, and she often wept in pain. Her mother-in-law showed little pity on her. Narsiah, though, was sad, and often rebuked his wife for such behaviour. Malliah, who visited his daughter often, could not say anything now that she was part of the household of another. He felt helpless. Narsamma got to rest only when her father-in-law was home. She was about twelve when Narsiah decided to take her to his son.

Ramaswamy was surprised to see his father visiting him with his wife and sister.

'Father, what's the matter? You've come so suddenly!' Ramaswamy said, taking the trunk from his wife.

'Nothing. How long are you going to stay without your wife?' Narsiah smiled at him, but Ramaswamy detected a gravity in his father's smile.

'What's the matter, Ayya? Why have you brought her here?' he asked again, looking at his wife. 'Who will help Amma?'

Narsiah said, 'Did you marry her for your amma?' And turning serious he said, 'Look at the poor girl. How she's been harassed by your mother! I can't bear to see her working the whole day without rest. You take care of her now.'

Ramaswamy was silent. He knew his stepmother well and felt sorry for his wife. He turned to look at her as she stood in a corner, chatting with his sister. Despite what he said to his father, he was glad that his wife had come to live with him. The two young girls went around the house looking at the things in the kitchen while his father rested. Narsiah stayed a couple of days, making arrangements for whatever the young couple needed, and then left, leaving Pentamma with them.

A new life began for Ramaswamy and Narsamma. Ramaswamy took his wife and sister to the marketplace and other areas of the small coal town. Narsamma, shy till now, began talking to him whenever they were alone, and later even in the presence of his young sister. Freed from her mother-in-law's cruel regime and from the heavy work that she had been made to do all day, she felt relieved. Now she happily cooked and kept house for the three of them.

One evening, seeing how tired her husband looked as he came in, she gave him a glass of water. Ramaswamy, instead of taking the glass, held her hand and pulled her to him. It was the first time he had embraced her; Narsamma wanted to withdraw, but he held her close. His touch sent shivers through her. Holding her tight, he asked, 'Where is my sister?' Struggling to release herself, she said, 'She's at the neighbour's.' Hearing Pentamma's footsteps, she pushed him back and ran out of the room.

She could not forget that touch, though. She looked at him from the inner room through the corners of her big eyes, seeing as if for the first time the fair, tall man with thick, black hair. She noticed that he had very attractive eyes. His body was strong, sturdy and well shaped. He had a good sense of dressing and changed into a spotless white dhoti and a nice shirt when he returned from work.

After dinner, Narsamma was busy cleaning the dishes. From time to time, she looked at her husband, who was trying to make Pentamma sleep early. Making sure she was asleep, he slowly turned off the flickering kerosene lamp and quietly took his wife into his arms.

Narsamma woke up feeling very different the next morning; she was not able to get up as early as she usually did. She had changed – the night's experience had left her strangely hesitant to even go out into the yard. Looking at her husband who was still asleep, she finally got up and adjusted her sari and went out to the front yard to sweep it clean. She was not her usual self, and frequently looked at her husband. Ramaswamy, who was supposed to leave for work early, did not get up in good time and had to rush. As he left the house, they smiled confidentially at each other.

Two months later, Ramaswamy received a promotion and transfer order. He was now posted at a station, Dharur, in the Secunderabad–Wadi section. He had also been promoted to the post of pointsman. He felt that his wife had brought good luck with her. They left within a week.

Dharur was a small station with just one railway line and a loop line. There were just a few railway quarters, close to the railway station, in a row. Ramaswamy and Narsamma's neighbours were Sudras – a pointsman with his family – on one side and an older untouchable couple on the other. Narsamma sometimes took help and advice from the older lady. Ramaswamy had different responsibilities now. He no longer had to go round the houses of guards and drivers, carrying heavy boxes on his head. His job was to signal to the up and down trains, light the lamps of the outer and home signals and perform other odd tasks like doing the domestic work at the stationmaster's house. He found this easy and, as before, he would read whenever he got the time. The stationmaster, a young upper-caste man, was surprised to see Ramaswamy reading, and treated him differently from the rest of the subordinate staff, most of whom were illiterate.

It was morning. Ramaswamy was away at work when Narsamma started retching. She had a pain in her stomach, and lay curled on the ground. A worried Pentamma rushed to the neighbour's house and brought the older lady in to take a look at Narsamma. The woman observed Narsamma carefully and smiled.

'There's nothing to worry about. It happens.'

Narsamma said, 'I am even throwing up water.' She felt exhausted.

The lady said, 'Don't worry, I shall send some rice gruel. Try to drink it. Even if you vomit, don't worry. You are going to be a mother.'

When Ramaswamy came home, Pentamma ran to him, 'Brother, sister-in-law is vomiting. She is pregnant.'

Ramaswamy beamed at his wife, who shyly smiled back at him. He now spent more time with his wife. He would get fresh toddy for Narsamma since it was one of the few things that she did not throw up.

On hearing the news, Malliah arrived with a large bundle of eatables: corn, peanuts and other cereals, all fresh from the harvest. He was elated that he was to become a grandfather. Narsamma was overjoyed to see him and ran into his arms. Malliah's eyes too were damp with joy. However, she could not eat anything her father had brought; only rice gruel and toddy agreed with her. Even the smell of oil made Narsamma nauseous, and it was Ramaswamy who now did the cooking.

Five months into the pregnancy, Narsamma went to live at her father's, leaving her husband and Pentamma behind. Malliah wanted the best possible care for his daughter, and called his sister to take care of her. He engaged an experienced midwife from his community to visit regularly. Narsamma's sisters too gave special attention to her.

Ramaswamy, now lonely, went out with his friends more often, drinking more than before. Initially, he would visit his wife on his days off, but over time he began to visit less and less frequently.

Narsamma's pregnancy advanced and she began to suffer from swollen feet. As the time drew near, Malliah's anxiety increased. The pains began one evening. Narsamma screamed with the pain. The midwife was summoned and she came running. She examined Narsamma. Noting that her navel was deep at the centre, she confirmed that the baby would come soon. She shouted for someone to keep hot water ready, and sharpened her sickle: it was with this sickle that she would sever the umbilical cord. Narsamma's aunt had the water boiling in a big earthen pot. The midwife asked Narsamma to push with greater force, and Narsamma, wracked by pain, cried out again and again as the baby wound its way out. The midwife pulled the baby out and cut the umbilical cord. The baby's cry was heard. The placenta was placed in a small earthen pot and buried in a corner. Wrapping the baby in a cloth, the midwife came out.

'Mallanna, your daughter has delivered a baby boy, and he is fine.'

Overjoyed, Malliah pulled out some coins from his pocket and poured them into her hands. This was his first grandchild.

It was now eleven days since the birth. So far, the mother and infant had been kept away from everyone, as was the custom. Today was a day of celebration. On this day, the new mother would bathe and wear new clothes and worship the well. After this ritual, she could move freely among everyone, and touch the cooking pot and other things in the kitchen. The infant too would be given a good bath and dressed in new clothes. A ritual warding off of evil followed, after which food and liquor were served to all the guests.

Narsiah, his wife and Ramaswamy were present at the celebrations. Narsiah was very happy as he held his grandson in his arms. The boy was fair like his father. The large black dot on his forehead and on each palm, under each foot, and the small black dot on his left cheek showed easily against his fair skin. Black beads were tied around his wrists. It was a rich celebration.

Malliah asked Narsiah, 'Bawa, I shall send Narsamma after three months. She requires rest now.'

'Yes, bawa, I share your thought,' replied Narsiah, looking at his grandson.

Ramaswamy was alone for the next three months. He began to drink regularly and sometimes drank heavily in the company of friends. He often had to go as a reliever to other stations, for up to fifteen days a month. This gave him additional earnings, and he began to spend all his money on his friends. He stopped reading too.

Ramaswamy was frequently sent to a station called Marpalli. There, he developed a friendship with Mogulappa, a porter in the railway goods shed who invited him for dinner now and then after a drink. Soon, the dinner at Mogulappa's house became a regular feature. Mogulappa had two brothers and a divorcee sister, Laxmamma. Laxmamma was fair, slim and beautiful, with big eyes and a well-defined nose. She made her own living. Although she lived with her brother, she would go to the fields to sow, weed and harvest. Laxmamma's husband had deserted her a few days after marriage. After two years of fruitless search, Mogulappa approached the elders of his community and Laxmamma was declared a divorcee. Since then, Mogulappa had been on the lookout for a husband for her. Laxmamma attracted the attention of every young man and many of them from her community were prepared to marry her.

Laxmamma developed an interest in Ramaswamy, preparing unusual dishes for him and treating him with special attention whenever her brother invited him. She took particular care of Ramaswamy and often participated in the conversation while serving food. She was enamoured of Ramaswamy's pleasing personality and would go to the station on the pretext of seeing her brother. Ramaswamy also began to take an interest in her. The two started meeting clandestinely. She would invite him for lunch in the afternoons when no one else was at home. Their intimacy grew, and for fifteen days a month, they spent most of their time with each other. It increasingly became difficult for Laxmamma to spend the rest of the fortnight alone.

The people of the community, especially the youngsters who had an interest in her, saw this and pressed Mogulappa to prevent his sister from having an affair with Ramaswamy. They said it would bring a bad name to the family. Not expecting this, Mogulappa was shocked and started avoiding Ramaswamy.

'Stop meeting Ramaswamy! People are whispering about your affair,' Mogulappa berated his sister, his tone harsh and determined. Laxmamma saw how serious he was, and was afraid. Lacking the courage to look her brother in the eye, she cried, 'Anna, I cannot live without him!'

'But he is a married man. You can't live with him,' Mogulappa tried to console her. But Laxmamma only wailed uncontrollably, and he was unable to say any more. He made up his mind to get his sister married as soon as possible.

Ramaswamy was on duty in Dharur and the down train had just arrived at the platform. He saw a woman getting off the train. It was Laxmamma. He rushed towards the bogie. It was a great shock to him. He had never expected her there. Hiding her face with the free corner of her sari, she was looking around for Ramaswamy. She saw him sprinting towards her. Making sure nobody was observing them, he almost ran as he took her out of the station, to a corner where nobody would see them together.

'Why did you come here? My master will sack me from my job if he sees you with me,' Ramaswamy said, worried.

Laxmamma's face was drenched in tears, 'Ramappa, I can't live without you, and my brother is serious about getting me married again.'

Ramaswamy tried to console her. He took her to a toddy shop, all the while trying to ensure that nobody observed them together.

'Look, Laxmamma, don't come here again. If the stationmaster sees you, he will fire me. Next month, when I come to Marpalli, I shall talk to your brother. Don't you worry,' he said as he made her sit under the cover of some bushes.

Laxmamma wiped her tears and smiled at him. 'Ramappa, I will only marry you, or give up my life.'

He sent her home by the next train.

Narsamma returned to her house in Dharur after six months. She now had the baby with her. She observed several changes in her husband: instead of reading books in his free time, he spent time with his friends and drank quite often. He was much more irritable than before. She attributed it to her own long absence.

Narsamma had brought Ramaswamy's brother Yelliah with her, since Ramaswamy was to be away for almost half of every month. Yelliah was a good boy. He had learnt to read and write with the help of his brother, and began to read the books that his brother had stopped reading. Ramaswamy had realized the importance of education when he joined as a box man in the railways. Having seen the lifestyle of higher-level and upper-caste staff, he wanted to ensure that his brother learnt English. He knew that this could fetch him a better job, a higher post. He took Yelliah to the stationmaster, who liked Ramaswamy. Yelliah would sit in the veranda with a slate, learning to write the English alphabet. He was keen to learn, and this made it easy for the stationmaster to teach him. Within a few months, the boy began to read and write simple words and phrases in English. It was the first

attempt in the Yelukati family to learn English, another attempt to
achieve a better life.

Narsamma conceived a second time very soon, but the second son
died immediately after birth.

Ramaswamy started avoiding going to Marpalli, requesting to be
allotted work at other stations. But his request was not honoured every
time, and each time he was in Marpalli, Laxmamma would pressurize
him to marry her.

Narsamma conceived for the third time, and this time her father
advised her to take extra care during the pregnancy. So, being as careful
as when she conceived first, he brought her home with him five months
into the pregnancy.

Ramaswamy sent his brother back to his father's, and was alone
once again.

'You are lucky. You have to work in Secunderabad on relieving duty,
a temporary transfer,' shouted the stationmaster at Ramaswamy, who
looked at him in surprise.

'Will I be able to work in such a big station, sir?' Ramaswamy
wondered.

'Don't worry, I know you can. Moreover, you are not illiterate.' The
stationmaster was happy for Ramaswamy.

Ramaswamy was glad that he would be able to spend time with
his father and learn from him. His only worry was that he would miss
Laxmamma and he decided to meet her before going to Secunderabad.
He decided to time it for his weekend off.

He got off the train at Marpalli railway station. He was dressed in
a spotless white dhoti and a white shirt with a blue blazer over it and
looked very smart. Mogulappa was surprised to see him.

'You are looking smart! Are you attending a wedding?'

Ramaswamy laughed, 'I just came to see you people.'

They sat talking in a toddy shop. Mogulappa said seriously, 'Bawa, you meeting my sister this way is not good. People are aware of your affair.'

'Don't worry, bawa,' Ramaswamy tried to make light of the situation.

'Don't take it easy. The community elders are thinking of expelling us if this continues,' said Mogulappa. Looking directly at Ramaswamy, he continued, 'My sister is adamant and says she will marry only you. Do something. I am worried.'

'Don't worry, bawa. This time I am going to Secunderabad on relieving duty and when I come back, I shall do what your sister wants.'

Mogulappa was satisfied.

They were just finishing their drinks when Laxmamma rushed to them, breathing hard. Ramaswamy's sudden appearance had taken her by surprise.

'When did you come?'

Thick, black strands of hair clung to her perspiring face as she looked at Ramaswamy. She looked more beautiful than ever.

Mogulappa left them together and headed for the station.

'You were supposed to come next week. I didn't expect you today.'

'Today is my day off. I came because I may not come to Marpalli for relieving duty this month.'

'Why? What's the matter?'

'I have to go to Secunderabad.'

'Oh, no!' Laxmamma was troubled.

'Don't worry, I shall come next month. I promise.'

It was a hot afternoon. Ramaswamy and Laxmamma were in Mogulappa's house. Laxmamma sat close to him, a worried look in her beautiful eyes.

'Appa! Everyone knows about our relationship. Do something.'

Drawing her close to himself, Ramaswamy said, 'I have already spoken to your brother. Don't worry.'

Both were besotted with each other and couldn't restrain themselves any longer.

Later, spent and exhausted, they sat quietly till a sudden sound outside made her pull herself away hurriedly. She said in a low voice as she set her sari, 'Please marry me at the earliest before something happens. We have to avoid meeting like this.'

Secunderabad had a very large railway yard, and many tracks. It was a new experience for Ramaswamy. The first day, he was afraid of standing between the bogies that needed to be coupled. His father helped him, teaching him the techniques, and even requested the muqaddam, the supervisor of pointsmen, to help his son. In three to four days, though, Ramaswamy was an expert at the job. He made new friends, and they would often meet in the evening to drink. He developed a taste for stronger alcohol.

It was a fateful day in Ramaswamy's life when he was implicated in a case of theft. One of his friends had stolen a bottle of liquor from a carton in a wagon and was caught. Ramaswamy was standing by his side, and though he had no role in the theft, he too was taken for interrogation. On hearing the news, Narsiah rushed to the police station. He fell at the feet of the police inspector, pleading with him to release his son. Some railway officials who had a good opinion of Narsiah also asked the police to let Ramaswamy go. But theft was a serious crime, and Ramaswamy was dismissed from service. Narsiah was distressed that his son had lost his job, but glad that he had been saved from going to jail.

On the way home he said, 'Son, don't worry. We shall meet Franklin Sir tomorrow. He will help you.'

Ramaswamy was silent. He had lost his job. Worse, he had hurt his father. He was extremely disturbed and cursed himself for falling into bad company. He did not know how he would face his father-in-law, or meet his wife who was expecting another baby. How would he raise his family without a job? His eyes filled with tears. Narsiah saw his distress and tried to console him.

They reached home. His stepmother had heard the news.

'Welcome, Son. You did a great job! Sit at home while your father feeds you and your wife,' she shouted at Ramaswamy as he entered the house. There was contempt in her voice.

Narsiah was furious. 'Shut up! Yes, I'll feed them!'

Seeing her husband so angry, Ramakka fell silent. Narsiah did his best to make his son forget what had happened and assured him that he would get back the job he had lost.

The next morning, Narsiah took Ramaswamy to Mr Franklin, the assistant personnel officer. He had dressed in his uniform and wore a turban, as was the protocol when meeting higher officials. He was very tense as he walked across the office veranda. Mr Franklin was a young British officer, and nice to the Class IV employees, often helping them in times of need. Class IV employees were seen at his office more often than other cadres, to whom he rarely granted personal appointments. Ramaswamy stood in a corner, his head down. His father-in-law, Malliah, who had come as soon as he had heard the news, stood by his side. When the officer called out for him, Narsiah rushed in and fell at Mr Franklin's feet.

'Hey! Get up, what's the matter?' shouted Franklin.

'Sir, my son is innocent, please pardon him,' cried Narsiah.

'Tell me what happened.' He was impatient.

'Dora, my son was dismissed from service yesterday ...'

'Oh! That fellow ... what's his name?'

'Ramaswamy, he's my son.'

'I remember, but it was a serious case. Thank God he was not sent to jail!'

'Dora, have mercy on him. He has a wife and children. You were the one who gave him a job.'

'Call the fellow in,' he said, and turning to look at Ramaswamy, he shouted, 'What's wrong with you? You're troubling your father who is a nice man. Get lost! You won't have a job with us again.'

Narsiah gestured to his son to leave. He fell at Franklin's feet again, weeping.

'Sir, you are our God. Have mercy on him. He did not steal. He just happened to be standing there when it happened.'

'Get up, Narsiah. What you say may be true, but the case is serious.'

Narsiah looked at him, still pleading with his eyes.

'Look. Let him not be seen around here for a month. Bring him after that, and I shall see how I can help.'

Narsiah came out of the office and joined his son and Malliah, who were anxiously waiting outside.

'What did the Dora say?' asked Malliah, very worried.

'Don't worry, bawa, he asked me to get in touch with him after one month and warned that Ramaswamy should not to be seen around these parts till then.'

They left the office with sighs of relief.

Narsiah sent his son to Jangaon where his uncles lived, and cautioned him not to go anywhere near the railways.

Narsamma gave birth a third time. It was a baby boy again, and the infant was healthy. This time, there wasn't much happiness in the family; Ramaswamy had seen his son, but was very tense. Narsamma was sad to see him so worried and apathetic. It was a difficult situation for Ramaswamy; he was an exile, making an effort to remain unobserved. It was miserable to be without work and to be bound to the house. He spent his time with his books.

A month later, Ramaswamy stood waiting anxiously outside Mr Franklin's office while his father was inside.

'Mr Narsiah, it is because of you that I am taking the risk of giving him a job,' said Mr Franklin.

'I am indebted to you, sir,' replied Narsiah and fell at the officer's feet.

'But see that his name is changed. I cannot take him on with the same name.'

'I have to change his name, sir?'

'Yes, tell me, what name shall I write?'

'His name shall be "Baliah Ankus", sir.'

'Call him in.'

Ramaswamy stood before the officer with folded hands. His father gestured to him to fall at Mr Franklin's feet.

'I am taking you back this time. Do your job sincerely. A slight mistake and you will lose your job for good.'

'Yes, sir, I promise,' said Ramaswamy.

After this day, Ramaswamy was known as Baliah. It was like starting a new life. He had a new name, Baliah Ankus, Ankus representing the name of a fictional father. He resolved not to be the cause of any trouble for his father in the future; his father's worry had caused him more anguish than the loss of job.

A big feast was held at Narsiah's house to celebrate Ramaswamy's reinstatement.

※

Baliah was posted to a remote station between Secunderabad and Wadi. This was intentional; nobody there knew of his history. Except a few old associates, everyone now called him Baliah. As Baliah, his career started afresh, and he once again devoted a large part of his time to reading and working. He kept away from making friends who could cause trouble and from strong drink, but he couldn't forget Laxmamma. He married

Laxmamma through an uncommon practice known as cheere raika. In untouchable and lower Sudra communities, marriage between a divorced woman or a widow and a married man or a widower is permitted. Baliah and Laxmamma lived together when he was posted to stations where very few members of staff were at work.

This lasted only a few weeks, though, for Baliah was posted to Secunderabad again. He did not like going back to the place where his career had taken a bad turn, but he couldn't help it. When not at work, he restricted himself to the house and engaged himself by reading or spending time with his brother. Baliah deliberately avoided his old friends. On his days off, he visited his wife and spent time with his children. The older son, Balraj, was now a toddler attempting to walk on his own. The younger son was three months old and had been given a rare name, Abbasayulu: a combination of the names Abbamma and Sayamma, the former being the name of Baliah's mother, and the latter of Narsamma's grandmother.

Narsamma had by now spent almost six months at her father's, and was insistent about returning to live with Baliah. Expecting her to join him very soon, Baliah made it clear to Laxmamma that she could not live with him on a regular basis. However, he would go to Marpalli and live with her for a few days every once in a while. Since the two had married, the people of Narsamma's community no longer objected to their relationship.

There was a sudden call for Narsiah one day: a man was shouting for him, his face pale and worried, his breath heavy. He was drenched in sweat; he had obviously been running hard. Narsiah was suddenly very worried. He looked enquiringly at the man, and the latter burst out, 'Your son Baliah has been taken to hospital! It was a serious accident; he fell under the wheels of a moving bogie.' A shocked Narsiah ran to reach the railway hospital at Lallaguda. Everyone seemed to be talking about the accident, but no one seemed to know in what condition Baliah was. Nurses were hurrying in and out of the operation theatre. Narsiah stood motionless and mute at the door. A doctor called out to him, asking him to go into the adjacent casualty room, for blood was needed. Baliah had suffered a deep cut on the right thigh and there had been heavy loss of blood. One of Baliah's colleagues told Narsiah that Baliah had slipped, falling away from the tracks, just after he had coupled two bogies. His right leg had got stuck under a moving wheel, and although the engine driver had immediately applied the brakes, the wheel had torn away a part of the flesh and left a deep cut on Baliah's thigh.

The surgery lasted almost four hours. Considering Baliah's health, the doctors felt that he would recover quickly. Narsiah was allowed to see Baliah through the glass door of the intensive care unit. It was a frightening scene: his son's face was covered with an oxygen mask, and he was being given blood from a bottle. He was still unconscious, and Narsiah could not bear to look at him for more than a few seconds. His eyes filled with tears, and for a moment he felt as if he was assuring Abbamma that their son would be all right.

Narsiah was sitting outside the hospital with his wife and Yelliah when Narsamma arrived with her father and children. Narsamma's eyes were red and swollen from crying and she broke down again when she saw her father-in-law. She did not know what to think when she saw her unconscious husband on the other side of the glass door. She attempted to push the door open and go to his side, but the hospital staff stopped her.

'Don't cry, my child, he's all right,' Narsiah consoled her.

Narsamma stayed back in Secunderabad with her parents-in-law, visiting the hospital daily. Malliah shuttled between Bibinagar and Lallaguda every day, procuring nutritious food for Baliah. He would also get him fresh toddy, which Baliah asked for and drank without the knowledge of the hospital staff. The wound was healing well and the crushed bark of the babul tree that was applied to his wounds by Malliah

was working wonderfully. Baliah was grateful for the care his wife and her
father were providing. Laxmamma and Mogulappa also visited Baliah
a few times, but this did not come to the notice of his family. A month
later, all that remained of his wound was a large, somewhat depressed scar
below his right buttock. Narsamma wheeled him out onto the veranda
of the hospital in the evenings. Gradually, he started walking with the
help of a stick. He was discharged after two months and advised rest for
another month. It was around this time that Pentamma got married to
a pointsman called Kanakiah.

A number of theories were advanced to account for the accident.
Relatives attributed it to his reading of books like the Ramayana and
the Mahabharata; they believed that this had brought Baliah bad luck.
It was a sin for untouchables to read and write! Baliah laughed on
hearing this.

It was nearly a year after the accident. Baliah was with his family again;
they were living at one of the many little stations. He spent a good
deal of time at home, playing with his children. Balraj, the older one,
entertained his father with the new words he was learning every day.
The younger one, Abbasayulu, would come crawling up, trying to
reach his father's arms, and both children then vied for his attention.
Narsamma was happy; she had found a great change in her husband
since the accident.

Three months later, Narsamma was expecting again. This time, she
decided that she would stay with her husband. After his accident, she
worried about his safety. As the pregnancy advanced, though, she had
a tough time looking after the two children, and Baliah decided to
send her to her father's. She left unwillingly, deciding not to stay away
for a long time, and making him promise to request the stationmaster
not to send him on relieving duties to bigger stations where shunting
was done.

But Baliah was soon transferred to a bigger station, Tandur, a place which had stone quarries all around. It was from here that the Shahabad stone was loaded into railway wagons. Since Tandur was a bigger station, more people worked there, and there were more railway quarters. This was the first time in Baliah's career that he had been posted full-time at a big station and was living in quarters where different classes of workers stayed. The size of the quarters differed according to the grade of the employee.

Baliah was alone when the Wadi–Parli Vaijnath passenger train arrived. Just as he was signalling for the train to move, he saw a woman walking towards him, her face covered with the free end of her sari. It was Laxmamma. Baliah recognized her only when she came closer. He was happy to see her, and asked her to sit until his work was done. They went to his quarters when his work was done.

While making rotis, Laxmamma asked, 'How long shall we live like this, Balappa?' She did not look at Baliah as she said this.

Baliah looked up: droplets of sweat covered Laxmamma's forehead, and she was pushing away the strands of hair falling on her face with the back of her hand.

'Let us wait for some more time. I shall call you at an appropriate time, when Narsamma is here.'

'I won't fight with akka. I respect her. But will she allow me to live with her?'

'She is a good woman. Let's hope for the best.'

'When will akka come?'

'In a month's time, I think. She said she would come soon this time,' said Baliah as he ate.

'Then I must go to Marpalli soon this time.' She was not happy about the prospect.

It was not uncommon for a man to have two wives, and the men in the quarters did not think too much of it. Also, Baliah was a new man and did not have many friends yet, so nobody asked him about it. The

women, however, whispered among themselves about the strange woman
in Baliah's quarters. When Laxmamma was at the well, drawing water,
an older woman asked her about her relationship with Baliah.

'I am Laxmamma, Balappa's second wife,' she replied, lifting a pot
of water to her head.

The other women looked at her curiously. 'She's beautiful,' one of
them said.

The news that another woman was living with Baliah slowly spread. It
reached Malliah's ears, but he would not believe it. It was only when a
friend of his, a gangman working in Tandur, confirmed it that he started
to pay any attention. He was shocked. Narsamma had, meanwhile, just
delivered a baby girl. Worried about his daughter's health, he decided
not to disclose anything to her yet.

When Baliah received news of his daughter's birth, he was very
overjoyed, and rushed to see her. Malliah treated his son-in-law in
his usual hospitable way. Narsamma's younger sisters, both of whom
were married, were also around. Yelliah, husband to Narsamma's sister
Laxmamma, lived in Malliah's house with them. He was an intalludu, a
man who adopted the family of his wife as his own and took the name
of her family. Baliah spent three happy days in their company. As Baliah
got ready to leave, Narsamma said, 'Ayya, I too shall come with you.'

Baliah looked at her and said, 'I shall come back and take you home
after twenty-one days.'

Until the late 1950s, the railways supplied groceries to its employees
throughout the country at subsidized rates. The railways, in those days,
was one of the best organizations to work for and took great interest in
the welfare of its employees. A railway wagon containing all kinds of
groceries would chug into every station in the first or second week of

every month, making available good-quality foodstuff to the employees. The last week of every month presented a stark contrast: a trader on a bicycle would often be seen in the railway quarters purchasing some of these groceries at throwaway prices: despite resistance from their women, many of the men who had no money for drink at the end of the month would sell their groceries to this trader.

Baliah was busy collecting his groceries from the wagon and putting them in a sack when he heard someone calling: 'Baliah, your wife, children and father-in-law are waiting at your quarters.'

Expecting his wife and children at any time, Baliah had already sent Laxmamma away. However, he had not expected Narsamma to return so soon, and certainly not with his father-in-law accompanying her. He wondered whether his father-in-law knew about his second wife. As he approached, he saw his wife and father-in-law in deep conversation. Seeing him, they abruptly stopped their discussion. They exchanged greetings. Baliah and Malliah fell silent while Narsamma began to feed her baby. The house was quiet except for the children shouting and playing with each other. Malliah wanted to avoid a confrontation with his son-in-law, and did not to raise the issue of the second wife.

Baliah was happy around his children and spent a lot of time with them. Narsamma gave them special attention, and they were always neat and clean. She would dress her children like upper-caste children, with silver bracelets and gold earrings. She looked like a caste Hindu woman herself, but for the tattoos on her hands that had been made when she was very young.

Children wearing gold was a privilege of the upper castes. The untouchables who lived in the railway colony enjoyed the same freedom as the higher castes. There wasn't any social restriction here. In colonial times, cantonment areas and railway colonies were 'free zones' for untouchables, where they could aspire to better social lives, and earn their livelihoods like caste Hindus. The economic opportunities were similar for both the touchables and the untouchables. Although the caste Hindus might have practised untouchability privately, they could not impose it at the workplace. Unlike in the villages, untouchables were not forbidden from drawing water from the public wells. But the caste Hindus still tried to avoid contact with the untouchables for fear of pollution, and both would not draw water at the same time – that would have meant touching each other's buckets! The untouchable women were slowly transforming their lifestyles too – bathing every day, and grooming their children well.

In the old order, untouchable women and men had a dress code, and were identifiable by their clothes. The women wore their saris in a way that only covered them up to the knees. They had tattoos on their hands and chin. The men wore dhotis that barely covered their thighs, and were not allowed to present themselves in front of caste Hindus wearing footwear. Untouchables in railway colonies openly defied such social customs, and began to sport clothes similar to those worn by caste Hindus. The women began to wear their saris in such a style that their ankles were covered, and they could afford to wear gold jewellery.

This time, Narsamma lived with Baliah for a relatively longer period before she was again with child, and it was only in the ninth month of the pregnancy that she left for her father's house.

It was the mid-1940s and the country was heading towards political independence. The Indian National Congress was active all over the country, save in a few pockets. In the princely state of Hyderabad, the Congress party existed along with the Communist Party of India. Two kinds of struggles proceeded simultaneously: a peaceful movement for political freedom, and an armed struggle against the feudal lords (promoted by the communists). The nizam's domain was the largest princely state in India, and included parts of present-day Karnataka and Maharashtra. Mir Osman Ali Khan, the last nizam, was not prepared to lose the state of Hyderabad to the Government of India if the country gained independence. His military forces, the Majlis-e-Ittehadul Muslimeen, or the razakars, were led by an able commander, Kasim Razvi. Terror was used to frighten people into giving up the struggle for freedom. Arson, rape and looting of Hindus was widespread. While many untouchables converted to Islam in their search for self-respect, many others, including Hindus who were not untouchables, were forced to convert to the nizam's religion by the razakars. Revenue and police officials offered incentives such as a pair of new white robes, food, and even land, in some cases, to aid conversions. Many untouchable families were converted en masse; a single mullah would convert the entire community in one go. The women often refused to wear the white saris offered to them – white being the colour of widowhood in Hindu culture – or to remove the pustelu, the sacred symbol of their married status, from their necks. The officials would ignore this and report to the nizam the 'success' of the conversions.

The feudal lords were greatly threatened by the armed struggle for independence. Arson and robbery became widespread in the villages, especially in the years 1946–47. Entire villages suddenly emptied out upon hearing that the razakars were coming. Women formed protective groups, always carrying household knives and even chilli powder to throw into the eyes of the attacking razakars who would ask them to strip naked or dance and sing for the razakars' entertainment or even rape and kill them in the presence of their men. Many Hindu men tried to disguise themselves as Muslims by sporting beards and wearing kurtas. As such, stripping them to see whether they were circumcised became the order of the day. For the Muslims, as for the Jews, circumcision was demanded by religion. If they were found out, the Hindu men were stabbed to death. Civil war broke out in Telangana.

Narsamma was in an advanced stage of pregnancy and on her way, this time, to her sister's house in Anantaram for her delivery. Her other siblings, Laxmamma and Ramiah, were accompanying her. They set out on foot from Bibinagar early in the morning. Little Bachamma was seated on Sayamma's shoulders, and Abbasayulu on Ramiah's. Balraj was walking with them and sometimes cried to be carried. They had just left a village, Gudur, and were within a mile of their destination when a group of people ran past them, shouting that the razakars were in Gudur. They had to hide quickly, for Narsamma was unable to walk fast. Seeing a fully grown cornfield, they left the road and entered it. Hidden among the thick, tall plants, they were invisible to people on the road. It was a hot afternoon; Ramiah uprooted a few plants to make room for Narsamma to lie down and Sayamma spread out a sari for her. Narsamma was breathing heavily now. Her feet were swollen and she was in much pain. Ramiah ran into the village and brought a midwife who examined her and said that Narsamma would take another two or three days to deliver the child.

'But she's in a lot of pain,' said Sayamma.

But the midwife was sure. 'No, they are not labour pains. She has had a long walk and so the pain.'

Sayamma heaved a sigh of relief. They remained there, letting Narsamma rest.

It was twilight, and a continuous tapping of shoes was now audible. It was the razakar soldiers on the road. Narsamma and the others were frightened, quiet and motionless now, almost holding their breath. One group, then another, and another, was heading towards Anantaram. They decided to spend the night in the cornfield. They sat awake most of the night, Ramiah with a stout stick in his hand.

Baliah was on relieving duty again. Laxmamma was in his house in Tandur. Everyone, including Narsamma, now knew about Baliah's second wife; she also knew that she would be with her husband in her absence. Both Narsiah and Malliah knew, but did nothing about it. They left it to Narsamma's discretion. Laxmamma's brother visited

Baliah regularly to share a drink. Baliah, although he enjoyed the drink, found it difficult to keep this up on his salary. Apart from his regular work, he began to work part-time as a hamali, carrying goods from railway wagons into trucks, and from trucks to railway wagons, in his free time. Laxmamma was now extremely happy: she had conceived. Baliah was happy too, but he was worried, for he was now faced with the prospect of maintaining two wives and their children on his meagre salary.

Narsamma gave birth to a baby boy and they called him Narsimlu. She returned to Baliah after a month, not spending much time at her sister's place. Mogulappa took Laxmamma away before Narsamma's return. Six-year-old Balraj helped his mother, taking responsibility for the new baby when his mother was busy in the kitchen.

Baliah was now transferred to Vikarabad. He had to find a balance between the two women, for Laxmamma also joined him soon with her baby boy, named Anjiah. The two women fought often, though Narsamma was calm by nature, and tried to avoid unnecessary disputes. Baliah often stood up for Narsamma during the quarrels since he felt that it was she who had been on the losing side – Laxmamma had come to live in Narsamma's house. The problem eased when Laxmamma, understanding Baliah's feelings, accepted the situation. They now started living amicably, and the women even became affectionate towards each other. They would share the housework and drink toddy with Baliah in the evenings. Laxmamma would help with the children, and Balraj became close to Laxmamma, calling her chinnamma (younger sister of one's mother). It was as if the children had two mothers.

For Baliah, though, it became very difficult to support his family on his income. Both women realized this. They began to work in the fields, carrying their infants with them, but leaving the other children at home in Balraj's care. Laxmamma, with her experience, found it easy, but it was tough for Narsamma at first, for she had never worked before. However, she learnt all the tasks from Laxmamma.

Although Baliah was worried about his eldest son's education, he could not send him to school. Not only was he frequently transferred, Narsamma needed Balraj's help to look after the younger children while she was away in the fields. Baliah taught his son the basics of Telugu at home.

In Vikarabad, a good number of untouchables worked in the railway station and the goods shed. They met during festivals and other social events. These people held Baliah in high regard and often sat around him as he read out from the newspaper on their demand. They were very proud of this man from their community who could actually read! Baliah, though, felt acutely his lack of formal education and wanted his children to be educated in school.

It was the month of June in 1945. Abbasayulu, Baliah's second son, was now seven, and Balraj nearly nine. Balraj was needed at home, but Abbasayulu at least could receive some formal education. It was with this thought that Baliah brought Abbasayulu to Secunderabad, deciding to admit him into the school at Lallaguda established by the railways. Lean and tall for his age, the boy looked decidedly rustic in his silver bracelets and gold earrings. He went barefoot, and held his father's hand tightly as they walked into the school. He looked fearfully around him as his father led him towards the headmaster's room. It was all very strange for him and he felt as if he had entered a new world. Some boys were playing in the school grounds, while many others were in their classrooms: all of them wore the same white and blue uniform. The boys looked at him strangely, laughed at him: Abbasayulu looked funny to them.

The headmaster of this school was a man named M.K. Narsimiah. He had an impressive personality, and always sported creaseless jodhpurs and well-shined shoes. He came to school in a Morris Minor. A strict disciplinarian, he would stand on the sprawling grounds after the daily assembly and take a careful look at all students as they filed into their classrooms, detaining the ones he found untidy. Children of all categories of railway employees were students in this school. Many of them belonged to the Sudra community and a few to the untouchable community. Baliah, who was in his uniform, saluted the headmaster even as his son trembled and hid behind him.

'Sir, I am Baliah and I would like to admit my son in your school,' said Baliah, politely.

The boy's funny appearance made even the headmaster laugh aloud, but Baliah's obvious annoyance caused him to stop and control himself. He asked, in the same polite tone as Baliah had used, 'Where are you coming from, Mr Baliah?'

'I am from Vikarabad, sir. I am a pointsman.'

'Vikarabad? How will you send your son to school every day? It is half a day away.'

'My son will live here with my cousin.'

'That's okay, then. What's his name?' he asked, looking at the boy.

'He is Abbasayulu.'

'A strange name!'

Baliah did not answer, and the headmaster went on, 'Okay, Mr Baliah, he can come to school here, but see that his anklets and earrings are removed. And he will have to wear a uniform.'

Baliah grinned; he saluted the headmaster repeatedly as he left the room.

As soon as they stepped out of the room, Abbasayulu, awed and overwhelmed by all he had seen, tugged at his father's hand and said, 'Ayya, let's go home. I won't go to this school.'

Looking at his son's frightened face, Baliah placed his hand on his head and reassured him, 'No, Son, you have to go to school and study well. You have to become a big officer.'

It was Baliah's deepest wish that his children be educated and become high-ranking and well-respected officers in the railways. For this, he was prepared to work extremely hard. Whenever he met an official, he imagined his own children holding such a position one day. His father, who could have provided a home to his son, had recently been transferred away from Secunderabad. So he had decided to leave his son with his cousin Narsimha, a railway porter who lived close to the railway station in a slum called Chilkalguda.

This was to be the first time that Abbasayulu was going to live away from his family. Ready to leave, Baliah avoided looking into his son's eyes. He said to his cousin in a choked voice, 'Brother, take care of my son. He has never stayed away from us before.'

'Don't worry. I assure you of his well-being,' Narsimha soothed the distraught father.

Abbasayulu held his father tight and started crying loudly. Baliah was choking on his own tears but he did not yield. He was determined that his son should go to school, and controlling his emotions he softly consoled his son, 'Don't cry, my son. I shall come on each day that I have a holiday to see you. You must go to school.'

He turned his face away, wiping the tears that were flowing involuntarily down his cheeks. He had arranged for Abbasayulu's school uniform and books. He had also provided all groceries that he would require for a whole month. Narsimha's wife took the boy inside as Baliah left, looking over his shoulder repeatedly.

When Baliah returned, Narsamma was disconsolate. She wailed for her son, and Baliah's eyes dampened even as he tried to console her. Balraj and Bachamma also wept, and it was Laxmamma who calmed them down.

Baliah's cousin was a poor man working as a licensed coolie at the railway station and had a hard time maintaining his own family of four. It became a monthly practice for Baliah to send Narsimha the provisions needed for Abbasayulu. It was Balraj who carried the groceries for Abbasayulu every month – groceries that only lasted for a few days in that family. It was a difficult time for Abbasayulu since he had to go to school half-starved. But he was determined to study well, and was one of the best students in his class. Learning in the English medium was difficult at first, but Abbasayulu was an eager learner and picked up the language in a very short time. When he came home during his vacations, he would read his lessons aloud in English. This made Baliah proud and he would repeatedly ask his son to read aloud, although he himself understood very little English and did not know how to read or write in the language. When Abbasayulu read, he imagined his son as a stationmaster. His dream of educating his children was slowly coming true.

Thus was a boy of the Yelukati family admitted into school for the first time.

In those days, there were many occasions when cows, buffaloes and other cattle fell victim to speeding trains. The stationmaster would, at such times, depend upon the untouchable employees to remove the carcass from the rail tracks, for no caste Hindu would touch the dead animal. The untouchables saw it as an opportunity to get some meat – enough to last them a few days.

A pointsman ran towards the stationmaster, breathing heavily. 'Sir, the train has hit a cow and stopped at the outer signal.'

'Where's Baliah?' called the stationmaster.

The engine was sounding its horn continuously. A group of untouchables ran towards the tracks to remove the dead animal. Soon, the track and the wheels were cleared and the train departed. The dead animal was carried into the railway quarters. A group of people surrounded the carcass – women, children and men, all untouchables. Baliah and a few colleagues were also there, and they helped make way for a Madiga pointsman to reach the dead cow. The man carried a large knife. He was an expert in skinning animals. After his work was done, the meat was cut into pieces and sorted into heaps of different sizes. Baliah supervised the distribution of the meat. Smaller portions went to smaller families and larger ones to the larger families. The next day, neat ribbons of meat seasoned with turmeric paste were to be seen hung out on wires to dry behind all untouchable quarters.

Mogulappa frequently visited, and Baliah had to spend money on the drinks. Narsamma was unhappy. Spending on drinks was something the family could ill afford, given the rising cost of their children's requirements. She and Laxmamma were already toiling in the fields to supplement the family's income and meet essential needs. It was on the issue of money that quarrels flared up between Baliah and his two wives. He would lose his temper at times, and beat one or the other of them. On one occasion, Baliah beat Laxmamma badly. Her face was bleeding, but when Narsamma tried to intervene, she said, 'Let him beat me, Akka, he's gone mad. Balappa, kill me.'

Baliah was mad with anger. 'Bitch, get out of the house! I don't want you any more!'

Laxmamma took her six-month-old son in her arms and was walking out when Baliah snatched the boy from her hands.

'It's all right; keep your son with you. I am going,' she said and ran out in a fit, not looking back.

Narsamma was very worried. She waited anxiously for Laxmamma to come back. She spent the night taking care of the baby, who was crying for milk. She herself had an infant, and in feeding Laxmamma's baby, she sometimes left her own son half-fed. She tried to convince Baliah to bring her back, or to take her son to her, but he was adamant and would not listen. More than a month passed, but Laxmamma did not return. With two suckling infants to look after, it was a difficult time for Narsamma. She fed Laxmamma's son her own milk while her son, who was a little older, was at times fed toddy.

Laxmamma never returned, nor did Baliah ever call her back.

Narsamma was kind-hearted. She had always been patient with

Laxmamma and treated her as her sister, despite the fact that her father Malliah was critical of her behaviour. Now, whenever he visited, he tried to talk her into sending Laxmamma's son away. But Narsamma raised Anjiah, Laxmamma's son, as her own. Anjiah too became very attached to Narsamma. She was bringing up 'twin' boys.

Balraj, at ten, was of immense help to Narsamma during this difficult time. He had begun to do odd jobs for the family, helped his mother in household tasks, and looked after the younger children when Narsamma was busy. He greatly enjoyed listening to her sing folk songs while he ground the flour and she went about her other tasks in the early hours when the rest of the family was still asleep. And when he went to Secunderabad to deliver the groceries, Balraj always gave his brother a few annas that he had saved from the money he earned.

Baliah was thankful that his son from Laxmamma was so well cared for by Narsamma. He now became more committed to and concerned about his children and gave serious thought to their education. His one great regret was that he could not send his eldest son to school.

Baliah was a highly disciplined man now. His commitment at work and respect for higher officials had always been great, but at the same time he was highly intolerant of officials who ill-treated the subordinate staff. He told his superiors to expect respect only when they gave respect; there had to be reciprocity. The officials would address him as 'Baliah' rather than 'Baliga', an appellation they would have used for a subordinate. It was now known in the railway circuit that Baliah would not have borne this patiently. He objected to officials addressing their subordinates with contempt. He also politely refused to do the personal work of the stationmasters, such as going to the market or taking their children to school, or washing their clothes. Because of this perceived insubordination, he was transferred many a time, but Baliah never had any regrets. It was after one such incident, in fact, that Baliah was transferred to a small station, Ghanpur, near Kazipet, on the other side of Secunderbad. He left his family at Bibinagar and reported for duty at the new station.

The station he now worked in had an assistant stationmaster, Mr John, a muscular young man and a boxer. Mr John was eager to show off his boxing skills but had not so far found a man who knew how to box, or even a man strong enough to test himself against. When he saw Baliah, the new pointsman, Mr John thought he was a wrestler, and that he could practise boxing with him.

'Arey Baliah, you look very strong. Can you fight with me?'

Baliah retorted strongly, 'Mr John, please stop using the word "arey". It's derogatory.'

'What! Are you an officer, then?'

'No, but you have no right to disrespect me. I am not your slave, and both of us are railway employees.'

'Are you trying to teach me? You ... a pointsman! Hit me, if you are a man,' he said, hitting Baliah on his face. Baliah lost his temper and catching hold of Mr John's hair with his left hand, hit him on his face hard with his right hand. It was a strong blow, and Mr John fell unconscious on the platform.

A passenger train was at the outer signal whistling for a 'line clear' that only a stationmaster or assistant stationmaster could provide. Two of the pointsmen carried Mr John into the station and tried to revive him by sprinkling water on his face. In a little while he got up and, wiping his mouth, gave the signal. The train was delayed, though, and after an enquiry into the incident, Baliah was transferred once again. The news, of course, had spread like wildfire in Ghanpur, and everyone condemned the assistant stationmaster's behaviour.

This time, Baliah was transferred to Sanatnagar, a small station close to Secunderabad, where Narsamma and the children joined him.

※

Narsamma had five children to look after now. One day, she was pleasantly surprised to see her father-in-law walking towards them. Taking his bag from him, she handed him a mug of water for his feet.

'How are you?' Narsiah asked, as he washed his tired feet.

'I am well. How are Mother-in-law and Yelliah?'

'Attamma is fine. And Yelliah has found a job – he's been appointed as pointsman.'

'Oh! That's great news!' She handed a glass of water to him.

Narsiah noticed the two little boys playing and asked, 'Who's the other boy?'

'Mama, he's also my son.'

'How is that possible? You are hiding something from me. My grandson is Narsimlu. Who's the other one?' he wanted to know.

'He's also your grandson, from Laxmamma,' she whispered.

Narsiah was surprised. Looking carefully at the boy, he could see the similarity between the child and his son. He was angry. 'Why did you keep him with you?'

'Mama, she ran away leaving behind her son, and he is your son's son, so I decided to raise him as my own.'

Narsiah was proud of his daughter-in-law. She was not just raising the boy, but giving him her love and affection, and more attention than her own son. As he took the other boy into his arms, his eyes filled with tears. Choking, he asked Narsamma, 'What's his name?'

'He's Anjiah,' replied Narsamma. She smiled as she took the boy from Narsiah.

Balraj came in just then. Narsiah was very happy to see his eldest grandson. Hugging him close, he exclaimed, 'Oh! You have grown so big! What are you doing these days?'

'Grandpa, I am at home helping my mother.'

'That's nice of you.' Turning to Narsamma, he said, 'Narsavva, your son has grown up. It's good that he is helping you.'

'Not only at home, he also does odd jobs outside. These days he goes painting.' Narsiah could see that she was sad as she said this.

'Where?'

'On railway bridges,' she said, in a choked voice.

'But why? It is dangerous ... working on bridges,' Narsiah was perturbed.

Baliah came in as Narsiah spoke, and Narsamma fell silent. Surprised at the sudden appearance of his father, but worried by the serious look on their faces, he said, 'Oh, no, Father, I have not forced him to go! He just doesn't sit at home when I go on duty.'

'Do you need his earnings?' Narsiah's tone was harsh.

'No, Father.'

That calmed Narsiah somewhat. 'Then stop him from doing such dangerous jobs, or else I shall take him with me.'

Baliah had denied to his father that they needed Balraj's earnings, but he knew they did. The family was growing in size, and they had to provide for Abbasayulu in Secunderabad too. Baliah's salary was not enough to make ends meet. Narsamma too went out to work in the fields, sowing, weeding and harvesting. Balraj, being the eldest son, had from a tender age taken up many responsibilities. He was very close to his mother and shared her work. When young, he had taken care of his siblings while she was out working, and now he shared the housework. Once Abbasayulu and Bachamma were old enough to share those responsibilities, he took it upon himself to find work outside the house. Neither Narsamma nor Baliah had wanted him to work at this tender age, but he wanted to help his family. As the family grew, Narsamma faced many challenges, and at every stage Balraj stood by her. Her wages and Balraj's supplemented the family income and helped ensure that the other children got education.

Now, Narsamma was expecting again, and would soon have to stop working. This time, she had decided that she would not to go to her father's, but deliver the baby at home.

⚹

Baliah worked in the nizam's state railway. This was a time when India was not a single unified country but a number of small states ruled by different rulers. The nizam ruled over the state of Hyderabad, which consisted of a large part of the Deccan. Mir Osman Ali Khan had the railway track laid right up to Bezwada (present-day Vijayawada) with his own money although Bezwada was not in his dominion but a part of British India. Bezwada was, in fact, a flourishing commercial town. The people working in the railways were not allowed to go beyond Yerrupalem, the last station before the border. Beyond this point it was British rule, and a traveller had to purchase British Indian currency – the Indian rupee or Kaladar rupee – which was of higher value compared to the Haali rupiya which was the currency of the nizam. A foreign exchange facility was provided at this station. There wasn't a free flow of people from one region to another, and the sociocultural aspects of these two regions were strikingly different. People crossing regions were easily identifiable by their clothes and the way they spoke. The people of Bezwada were almost frightened to talk to people under the nizam's rule. The medium also proved a problem; although the language Telugu was common to them, an Urdu flavour set the Telugu of the people belonging to Hyderabad apart.

Baliah had many friends in places like the 'running department', where drivers, firemen, coalmen and guards worked. These people would go right up to Bezwada, the terminal point of the train, although it was outside the limits of the nizam's railway. They often brought back edible oils, mangoes and other delicacies of a quality not available in their own area. Upon request, they brought such goods for their friends.

'When are you going to Bezwada?' Baliah asked his friend Narsiah. They were sitting in a toddy shop sipping their drinks. Narsiah was a fireman who frequently went to Bezwada on an express train.

'Why do you ask?'

'You must get me some mustard oil. We're going to have a new baby very soon,' said Baliah. Mustard oil was not easily available, but it was considered, as it still is, essential for massaging newborns, and as a laxative.

'My duty is on the express train, and that does not halt at Yerrupalem. I will not be able to get the money exchanged.'

Baliah took out a British Indian coin from his pocket. 'I have a rupee. Please get the oil. It is urgent.' It was all the foreign currency he had, but it was enough. Narsiah duly brought the mustard oil, well in time for the child of Baliah's – the first to be born in his own house.

They were now living in small railway quarters at Fatehnagar Gate. Narsamma was in labour. Baliah had rushed and fetched a midwife when the pains started. The children were sleeping in the neighbour's quarters, and one of their neighbours, a young woman, had set water boiling in a big pot. Narsamma was guiding the young lady even while in labour, and the midwife, a strong and sturdy woman ready with her sickle, asked Narsamma to push. It was the first time that Baliah was by his wife's side at such a time. He was pacing restlessly up and down outside the quarters when he heard Narsamma's screams – a new experience for him – and then the baby crying. It was a baby boy, the sixth child, and the author of this book. The midwife washed the baby and wrapped him in a piece of cloth, then asked Baliah to come in to see the baby. Baliah saw the baby that had just been born – his own child. He was intoxicated with joy: taking a few coins from his pocket, he drew them in circles around the baby's head to ward off evil spirits and handed them to the midwife. He decided to celebrate the event in a big way, inviting all their relatives.

On the twenty-first day, Baliah's small house was crowded with relatives. His father and father-in-law were chatting happily. The women were busy, some cooking for the feast in the backyard, a few inside the house, bathing Narsamma and applying turmeric paste on her body. Men sat around waiting for the toddy that Ramiah had brought in. Everyone had a sumptuous feast. Baliah's father named the boy Sathiah.

Over the next two years, Narsamma had two more children, a girl and a boy. The girl was named Lakshmibai and the boy Yadagiri.

It was now a large family; there were eight children in all. These were difficult days. Though he worked very hard, Baliah found it difficult to meet even the basic needs of his family. Apart from his job, he had also begun to work at a goods shed. Trans-shipment required labour, and he helped carry the heavy load from wagons to trucks and from trucks to wagons. Narsamma worked as an agricultural labourer, leaving behind her breastfeeding boy in Bachamma's care. She worked from early morning to late in the evening, and it was Bachamma who took the baby to Narsamma to feed the child each afternoon. Balraj, almost sixteen now, did all kinds of odd jobs to help the family's earnings.

Baliah's second son, Abbasayulu, was at the railway school in Secunderabad. Though he could not afford to send the younger children to the railway school where Abbasayulu studied, Baliah was determined to send them to schools wherever he worked. The three boys – Narsimlu, Anjiah and Sathiah – went to schools wherever Baliah was transferred. They often walked long distances to reach the primary schools, which were usually quite far from the railway stations.

The children often faced humiliation at school since they were the only children from the untouchable community attending school. They were made to sit separately and were not allowed to take water from the school pots; they had to go to a distant place, into the Harijanwada where the dwellings of the untouchables were, to quench their thirst. India had just become independent, but schools in the rural areas were as stubborn as they had always been.

Baliah was next transferred to a place known as Bonakalu, which is a part of the Andhra region. Its culture was very different from that of the Telangana region, where Baliah's family came from. Man tends to adopt the culture of the region he lives in, for his social life depends on this. Baliah and his family found themselves adjusting to this new culture. Hitherto, the children had called their father Ayya, but when he heard other children calling their fathers Nayana, Baliah insisted that his children call him Nayana too. It took them a long time to switch over to Nayana.

Here, the school was a mile away from the railway station. Baliah's three sons were the only untouchables in the primary school; they had been admitted by the schoolteacher only because of the stationmaster, to whom Baliah had made a special request. The three brothers had to walk a long distance early each morning to reach school. They brought their own gunny bags to use as mats as they squatted on the ground in a corner of the classroom. No other student would touch them for fear of pollution. When the teacher had to write on their slates, he would ask a Hindu student to sprinkle water on the slates before he touched them. There was no one to play with them and the brothers played among themselves. The Brahmin teacher wouldn't shirk from mercilessly beating these children for even the smallest mistake since he felt, as he repeatedly told them, that their presence polluted the class. Had it not been for the intervention of the local patel, he would have sent them away long back. The patels were the headmen of each village or town: one of them, called the police patel, maintained law and order, and the other, known as mali patel, was in charge of revenue and general administration. Baliah, as an employee of the railways, had the support of both patels.

The restrictions, humiliation, insults and discrimination meted out to his children did not deter Baliah from educating them. He advised his children that they neglect these insults and humiliations. Pursuing their education was, he maintained, the only way out of their misery and was necessary if they wanted to become masters in the railways. And this, Baliah – himself an ordinary Class IV employee – deeply wanted. Every evening he sat with them, and like a tutor, made them repeat what they had learnt in the classroom. When he was not around, Bachamma, his daughter, who had now stopped going to school, sat with them. Bachamma had gone to school while in Dharur and had studied up to the third standard. Baliah had wanted to send her to Vikarabad, where there was a girls' hostel, but his sister Pentamma strongly advised against it. But Bachamma played an important role in monitoring her brothers' education; she would make them sit down to study when her father was on duty in the evenings. She gave special attention to Sathiah who was young and needed help. She would laugh at his appearance when he returned from school, his dress soiled and his face smeared with dust. He looked like a buffoon, she said affectionately. He was so young that he could not even spread his gunny bag properly, and would never remember not to place his hands on the dusty floor. Nor could he remember not to wipe his face with his dusty hands, and thus always got his face smeared with dust. Bachamma would laugh at his funny appearance or get angry and scold or beat him, but she would give him a bath every evening. The three boys were always under the watchful eye and strict discipline of either their father or their sister.

It had been long since Baliah had gone to Bibinagar with his entire family. His father-in-law was very happy: his son-in-law had almost forgotten Laxmamma, and his daughter was once again happy and at peace with her husband. His grandchildren were going to school, and his second grandson was in a big school studying English. They had all come down for his son Ramiah's wedding; it was the last wedding in Malliah's house. It was a time of celebration. Baliah had nothing to do save eat and drink, and entertain his sisters-in-law. Baliah commanded the respect of everyone in Malliah's family, and was always given special attention. Malliah arranged to serve him toddy from a single palm tree. Rich as he was, he could afford this privilege, which was usually available only to the higher-caste Reddys and other landlords.

The wedding was grand. After the ceremony, Malliah arranged a visit to Yadagirigutta as he had vowed that he would visit the Narasimha Swamy temple after his son got married. The Narasimha Swamy temple, a famous hill temple at Raigir in the Nalgonda district of Telangana and about twenty miles from Bibinagar, is a well-known centre for pilgrimage. In those days, untouchables were not allowed to climb the hill but only allowed to offer prayers at one point at the foot of the hill, and they were assigned a route that was not used by caste Hindus. Four bullock carts were arranged. Rice, cereals and other necessities such as firewood and utensils were piled in one of the carts. A large sacrificial goat was tied to the cart, and when the cart set off, the creature walked along with the cart. The marriage party followed in the other carts.

It took over four hours for Malliah's caravan to reach Yadagirigutta. They bathed in an open well meant for untouchables, and housing the children in a choultry (as lodgings at pilgrim centres are called) meant for untouchables, the elders – including the bride and bridegroom – set off towards the foot of the hill. An untouchable butcher was always there, ready to perform the ritual. The man, after applying turmeric paste and vermilion to the goat's face, threw a bucket of water on it, upon which the creature shook its body vigorously. 'The god has accepted the offering; slaughter it,' shouted Malliah. The butcher cut off the goat's neck in a single stroke of the blade.

They stayed at the foot of the hill for three days.

After they returned, Malliah's sister made arrangements for a ritual known as vodi nimpadam or biyyam poyyadam. This ritual is performed immediately after the marriage of a son or daughter. It is an expression of happiness and joy towards already married daughters. In this ritual, each daughter is seated alongside her husband, and rice, dry coconuts, betel nuts and betel leaves are offered to them by three or five married couples. It is said to bring good fortune to the daughters' families. After this ritual, the parents bid farewell to daughters and sons-in-law, who then leave for their own homes. Malliah offered new clothes to all his daughters and sons-in-law.

Baliah's family reached home after seven days. The children had had great fun at their grandfather's. Narsamma had an opportunity to catch up with her younger sisters, and importantly, she had had complete rest from household work.

Balraj had turned eighteen. Baliah wanted to get a job for his son. He met Mr Franklin, who promised Balraj a job. Mr Franklin was glad that he had given a second opportunity to Baliah, who had turned out to be a good worker.

As expected, Balraj received a letter from the railways for an interview. It was for the post of a box boy, the lowest level in the railways. Like his father at that age, young Balraj was fit and sturdy. The interview went well, and a letter informing him of the posting was expected. Baliah was extremely happy, and although Narsamma was happy too, her heart was heavy that Balraj, who was her great strength, would perhaps have to move to another place.

It was a coincidence that Balraj was posted at Bellampalli, the very place his father had started his career in. He had to report there after undergoing a fitness test in the railway hospital at Lallaguda. His mother was making preparations for his departure. He would use the same trunk that his father used to carry, keeping in it all the rations he required for one month. She spent at least an hour each day alerting him about the precautions he should take while living on his own. Everything was packed and ready at last. Everyone was charged with emotion. Narsamma's eyes were red and swollen with weeping, Balraj's younger siblings were disconsolate, and Baliah was trying to pacify everyone. Balraj was most worried about his mother and wondered how she would manage without him. The thought of leaving her made the tears roll down his cheeks. He bid goodbye to his mother and siblings and, accompanied by his father, left. Baliah's first son had secured a job in the railways: the third generation of the Yelukatis to make a livelihood in the railways.

They reached the Bellampalli railway station. It was a new place for Balraj. To Baliah, who had started his career here, the place appeared quite changed. He was visiting the place after eighteen years – Baliah tried to remember the place as it was in the days when he had started his career as box man. A new platform had been added and there were many new amenities for passengers. The yard had expanded, and several new tracks had been laid. Some of the steam engines had been replaced by diesel ones. It was a strange coincidence that his son was now joining service in the same position and in the same place. Baliah was unhappy that his son could not start in a better position than he had. Balraj picked up his luggage and the two of them headed towards the stationmaster's office. Baliah was in uniform, and this made it easy for him to introduce himself to the stationmaster and other staff. Balraj took out the order of appointment and politely handed it to the stationmaster. He was given temporary accommodation in a dormitory along with two newly recruited people. Later, Baliah met the stationmaster, who was the same man who had been the assistant stationmaster when he had worked there, and secured small quarters for Balraj.

The next day, father and son sat silently on a bench in one corner of the platform, waiting for the train: Baliah had to leave. He was sad that his son would be away from home, but he was happy that he would start earning and was about to live on his own.

'Be careful, my son, you should be punctual in your duty.'

'That's fine, Father.'

'You should respect your elders. And there is one more important thing that I would like to say ...' Baliah trailed off.

Balraj looked curiously at his father.

'Look, Son, stay away from bad company. You know, I would have ruined my life had your grandfather not saved me.'

'What?' Balraj looked at his father in surprise.

'I had fallen into bad company and spent much of my time drinking hard liquor, and lost my job. It is because of your grandfather that I am where I am.'

'Don't worry, Father. Have faith in me.' Balraj looked at his father, whose eyes were filling with tears. They got up as the train entered the platform.

Baliah waved to his son as the train left. Through his moist eyes his son was a blur, waving at him.

As Balraj returned to his dormitory, he felt a sudden loneliness: he was staying away from his family for the first time in his life. He was worried about his mother, wondering how she might be coping without him. She had prepared enough food for him to last two days. Untying the cloth bundle, he began to nibble on a piece of jowar roti. He imagined his mother grinding jowar while singing folk songs, and he could eat no more.

The next day was his first at work. Balraj had to go to the quarters of an Anglo-Indian driver to carry his box to the train. Balraj gently tapped at the door and heard a hoarse voice, 'Who is there? Come in.'

'It is me, sir, your box man.'

Balraj's voice was very gentle. He could see the man tightening his belt; he was fat, and was not wearing his shirt. Both arms were tattooed, and he had a brown moustache and sideburns. As Balraj stood at the doorstep, hesitating to enter the house, the man repeated, 'Hey man, come in. Are you new? What's your name?'

'I am Balraj, sir. I am the new box man.'

The man looked at him. 'That's okay. Take the box to my engine.'

Since he was an Anglo-Indian, he let Balraj enter right into his house, and helped him lift the heavy box on his head.

There were four box men in the station, two of whom were untouchables and two Sudras. The higher-caste drivers and Brahmin guards still preferred the Sudras to the untouchables when it came to carrying their boxes. But the untouchable box men gained entry and could move freely in the Anglo-Indian houses, a new experience for them. Thus Christianity embraced these outcasts into its fold and, in the form of the British administration and better opportunities, opened the doors of education for them.

Balraj was better at reading and writing than his father. He had started learning English on his own, and could write the names of railway stations. He even signed his name in English. He also had a pleasing personality. In no time, he became popular among the staff, especially with the drivers and guards.

In the beginning, everyone felt sad at Balraj's absence. Narsamma missed his presence and his help. Her daughter Bachamma took over the chores. But there was little time to worry for too long. Baliah was transferred to Sirpur Kagaznagar. This town was then, as it is today, well known for its paper industry. As usual upon each transfer, Baliah faced problems with his sons' schooling. This time, the three boys were admitted to the Government Primary School. Time flew, and soon it was the children's vacation. Narsamma being with child again, all of them went to Bibinagar, to Narsamma's sister, Laxmamma. Laxmamma was happy to see her sister and the children after so long. This time, Narsamma had a strange feeling in the final days of her pregnancy. She felt very heavy, walked slowly, and experienced difficulty in doing even light work. The midwife was called, and after examining Narsamma, she said that they should expect twins.

Malliah took special care of his daughter and refused to let her do any work. He was very anxious about her health, and plied her with good food. In the evenings he would sit with her and both would drink toddy. He requested the midwife to pay frequent visits until she had safely delivered the infants. Everyone was concerned since the delivery of twins was risky in those days. Even the midwife was worried. Narsamma's other sister Sayamma also came over from Anantaram to take care of her.

The delivery took place one evening, and under the care of the midwife and her two sisters, Narsamma safely delivered twin boys. Malliah, who was waiting outside, was relieved. Sayamma had no children of her own. Gently lifting one of the boys in her hands, she said, 'Akka, let this boy be my son.'

Narsamma laughed, 'Okay, take him. God gave me two sons, so I could give you one.'

Sayamma was delighted. She kissed the boy several times and declared that she had become a mother. They named the boys Ramu and Laxman.

Balraj had come to Bibinagar for the first time after getting a job. Malliah looked at him in surprise; he had grown stronger and was obviously more responsible. Balraj greeted him with a broad smile. 'Tatha, how are you?'

Malliah hugged him, 'My dear grandson, you have grown very big!'

On seeing her son, Narsamma broke down. She hugged and kissed him several times and enquired, 'Are you okay? You've become so lean! Are you not eating properly?'

'I am fine, Mother,' Balraj replied. He then looked at his twin brothers, and grew very excited. He held them one after the other and laughed with joy. 'They are so cute!' he cried, while their mother smiled at him.

In the evening, Ramiah, the uncle who had taken care of him when he was young, took him out for a drink of toddy under the palm trees.

※

Baliah was firm about maintaining a strict schedule at home. His children would be in bed by nine in the evening, and up at four in the morning. He would make them sit down to read after a wash. Anyone who felt drowsy would be made to wash his face again, and stand and read aloud. This taught his children self-discipline. In the absence of her mother, Bachamma took care of everything at home. She monitored her three school-going brothers and managed the two younger children Lakshmibai and Yadagiri. Soon, Narsamma was back in Kagaznagar, not with twins but with just one son, Laxman. With Baliah's consent, Sayamma had adopted the other son, Ramu.

Baliah's colleague Pochiah had a girl in mind for Baliah's son Balraj. The girl lived in Huzurabad. Baliah and Pochiah travelled to Huzurabad to meet the girl's father Rontala Gattiah who lived in Harijan Colony. Gattiah was a prominent Madiga holding three acres of land, and he had three sons and a daughter. His daughter went to school and his sons tilled not only their own land but also other land that they had taken on lease. Unlike most of their community, they were farmers and not agricultural labourers, and had a well in their own backyard. It was a prosperous untouchable family. Though it was a thatched house, it was spacious, with three rooms.

The men washed their feet at the well and sat with Gattiah on a mat. After exchanging the customary greetings, Gattiah asked, 'Which village do you belong to?'

Narsiah replied, 'We are from Vangapalli, but we work in the railways.'

'Oh! So you work in the railways ...'

'They get good wages. His son is an educated man,' said Pochiah.

'Do you consider our family unsuitable for your daughter because we work in the railways?' asked Narsiah impatiently.

'No, no ... I was just curious,' Gattiah tried to pacify Narsiah.

'Can we see the girl?' asked Baliah. They did not want to appear anxious, although, unknown to Gattiah and his daughter, they had already seen and liked the girl. They had caught a glimpse of her in her classroom through a school window overlooking the road.

'She has to come home from school. I've sent my son to fetch her,' smiled Gattiah.

Pochamma, Gattiah's daughter, was at twelve the most beautiful girl in the untouchable community. She was not very tall, had dark curly hair, a straight nose and big beautiful eyes; tattoos dotted her forehead and cheeks. She was fondly called 'Raya posu' by her family, the colloquial name of a temple deity called Raja Pochamma. Being the only girl in the family, she was pampered by her brothers, and knew little housework. She was good at her lessons in school, and her parents felt great pride when she read her lessons aloud. It was a happy family.

Narsiah and Baliah expressed their readiness to the proposed match. Gattiah's eldest son Malliah brought a big pot of toddy and all of them enjoyed a drink before parting. A few days later, Narsamma and Baliah's sister Pentamma paid a visit to Huzurabad and fixed the wedding date.

Balraj was eighteen and Pochamma twelve when they got married. Apart from all the brass kitchenware required, Gattiah gave one thousand and one rupees as dowry, a rare thing in untouchable families in those days. The bride stayed with her parents-in-law in Kagaznagar for a few months before she joined her husband at Bellampalli to start a new life, just as her mother-in-law had once done.

Narsiah retired from the railways and settled in Jangaon, his maternal village where he had a small house in the Harijan Colony. His younger son, Yelliah, lived in Bansilalpet, the oldest colony in Secunderabad where many people from the Madiga community live today. Yelliah, who had begun learning English under a stationmaster's tutelage, now knew good English. He too had joined the railways, and within a short time, was promoted to the post of shunting master, in the category of an officer. He was respected as well as popular, and was one of the first men from the community of untouchables to become a Class III officer. He was also the first person from the Yelukati family to reach this level. Baliah was very proud of his brother's feat, and now felt that his dream of his sons becoming officers was achievable after all.

Baliah was promoted to the post of muqaddam, a supervisor of pointsmen. Although this entailed a transfer to Nizamabad, he was pleased since the transfer was accompanied by a promotion. The place he was moving to was a fairly large city, one named after Nizam-ul-Mulk. The nizam had laid a metre-gauge rail track from Kacheguda to Manmad in 1905, and the Nizamabad station was about 150 miles away from Hyderabad on this route.

The family arrived at the Nizamabad railway station by train. It was a big station with a large railway yard, and the children, now in Bachamma's charge, were delighted and excited. Baliah reported to the stationmaster, who allotted them quarters in the big railway colony that held about a hundred quarters for employees of various categories. Their new quarters had a big neem tree in front, its leaves providing welcome shade in the hot sun. A little distance away, in a walled compound, were bungalows meant for stationmasters, permanent way inspectors (PWIs) and other officials. On the other side of the track, near the railway station, were big independent bungalows meant for the Class II officers.

Baliah's immediate concern now was to place the children in schools. As muqaddam he supervised the work of four pointsmen, but he was still a Class IV employee. However, he was very conscious of his clothing, and when off duty, he would wear a spotless white dhoti with an ironed shirt and a blue blazer over it. His thick black hair was always oiled and his bushy moustache well maintained. At the government primary school where he went to seek admission for his children, the headmaster thought he was a patel from the adjacent village. Narsimlu and Anjiah were admitted to standards three and two, and Sathiah was admitted into a railway primary school closer home, in the first standard.

Self-help was a requisite in their hard lives, and washing and ironing their own clothes was part of their daily life till the time they gained employment.

The younger children, Lakshmibai and Yadagiri, soon reached school-going age. Now, apart from Abbasayulu who was still in Secunderabad, Baliah had to send five children to school. It was an uphill task, and would not have been possible had his wife and daughter not pitched in. Within a year, Bachamma too started working in the paddy fields. Like many untouchable women, Narsamma would carry the infant Laxman to the fields while she worked. She would hang makeshift cloth-cradles from the branches of nearby trees and rock the child asleep while she worked, taking breaks to feed him.

Like the children of other railway employees, Narsimlu, Anjiah and even Sathiah began to contribute to the family. When they had time, they sold sugar-cane pieces to passengers on trains that stopped at the Nizamabad railway station. They would carry the pieces on their shoulders and shout their wares: 'Ganna ... Ganna ... ek anna mein ek.' Narsimlu was the smartest, making the highest sales; he would even board moving trains to collect money from the passengers and then get off. Narsamma would save this money in an earthen pot to use in case of dire necessity.

Nizamabad, being a large railway station, had many Class IV employees, mostly belonging to the Sudra and untouchable communities. The festival of Holi was jointly celebrated by these communities. This was one festival in which even people from other religions – like the Muslims – took part. Baliah, as the muqaddam, took a keen interest in the celebrations. He would lead a team of people and approach officers to collect donations to celebrate the event grandly. The children of the colony would begin to celebrate a week before the festival, going abo in groups singing Holi songs and beating drums in front of shops

The children were happy in the schools here since there was no segregation of untouchable students; all students sat on benches. Their uniforms were made out of the cloth provided by the railways to Baliah for his uniforms. Thick blue shorts were stitched from the cloth provided for his trousers and thin blue shirts from that provided for the turban. Narsimlu and Anjiah walked two miles through the town to their school. Sathiah, whose school was housed in a large building on the other side of the tracks, was taken to school by Bachamma. Of the three, Anjiah was a mild-mannered boy and faced no problem at school, and Sathiah was too young to be any trouble. Narsimlu, though, was rather naughty; he had many friends and would sometimes skip classes and play with them instead of attending classes. Knowing this trait, Bachamma would check with the school and punish him for such lapses, sometimes beating him or making him stand in the hot sun. It was her careful supervision that ensured that her brothers went to school on time, dressed neatly and carried all that they needed for their lessons.

Nizamabad was the place these three would recall when, as adults, they spoke about their childhood.

Unlike other untouchable students, they had a disciplined atmosphere at home. Under Baliah's strict eye, they were up at four in the morning to revise their lessons. In the evenings too, they would not go out to play once their father returned home: Baliah believed that too many games distract children from their studies. Narsamma too nurtured a lot of hopes for her children. Each morning, she would get up at four to grind the jowar and make nearly fifty rotis for the large family, to be eaten with dal or chinta pandu karam, a paste made of dry chillies and wet tamarind. Any other food was a luxury. She also worked part-time as an agricultural labourer when necessary.

The regular monitoring had an excellent effect: the three boys learnt to take their education seriously. They developed other habits too – bathing in cold water was one such habit that lasted them a lifetime.

collecting money, even though at times they would be chided by the shop owners. Narsimlu was the leader of a small band of children, and over the week they would collect firewood and other combustibles in one place. On Holi eve, they would arrange it in a big heap known as kamudu and light a bonfire to denote the burning of evil. They would sing and dance around the fire as the elders looked on and enjoyed their liquor. On Holi, they would smear colours on each other, celebrating the advent of spring and signifying the vibrancy of the new season.

'What, man, Balraj, congratulations!'

The stationmaster was addressing Balraj from his room, and Balraj entered it looking a little worried, almost suspecting that something had gone wrong. The stationmaster was smiling. 'Mr Balraj, you have got a promotion and transfer to Secunderabad. You are a lucky man!'

'Thank you, sir!' replied Balraj, at a loss for words. He came out of the room with a transfer order in his hands and a grin on his face. He had been promoted to the position of pointsman. He had not even dreamt of a promotion, and now he had not just got that, he had been transferred to Secunderabad too! It was nearly two years since he had joined the railways and now he had a six-month-old daughter, Padma. He almost ran home in his eagerness to share the news with his wife.

They soon moved to Secunderabad and rented a house in Chilkalguda. Abbasayulu, who had been living with his uncle, now joined them. He was in the pre-final stage of high school, and was very happy to stay with his brother, who took it upon himself to share the responsibility of his sibling. His wife Pochamma was hardly fifteen, but her dedication and sense of responsibility for the family was evident. Over a period of fifteen years, she helped maintain the large family as one unit, bearing seven children of her own in that time.

In the village of Anantaram, Sayamma, Narsamma's younger sister, raised her adopted son Ramu with the greatest love and care. She stopped working in the paddy fields to take care of the baby. Very soon, the boy came to recognize her as his mother, and this gave her great joy. She bought him the choicest clothes and procured toys from the nearby town of Bhongir. All of a sudden, when he was about a year and a half, Ramu fell prey to high fever. Sayamma rushed him to a doctor, but the treatment did not improve the boy's condition; instead, it worsened. Panicking, she took him to a sorcerer and to every person or place that people suggested. When the child died three days after falling ill, it was the saddest and darkest day in Sayamma's life.

'Son, you would have survived had you been with my sister! I'm the one that has killed you, my son ...' Sayamma's grief was uncontrollable, and she beat her chest and wailed loudly as she sat beside her beloved son's body. Seeing her sister Narsamma, she broke down, 'Akka, my son has left me and gone. God is merciless, Akka!' She was almost insensible as she held her sister tight.

Narsamma was in deep anguish and couldn't help wondering that she might have had both twins alive if she had not given the child away. But she tried to restrain herself. Although her grief was great, her sister's was much greater – her dream of having a child had come to an end. She tried to console her sister even as her own tears flowed. Baliah too broke down on seeing the dead child. But he controlled himself and began trying to comfort the two women.

The people of the community similarly bewailed the loss of Sayamma's child. Whispers were heard that the boy had died of sorcery.

'A sorcerer took my son's life, Akka. I know that man; God will break his head into pieces and take his life, and I curse him, Akka,' Sayamma broke down again.

It was a very difficult time. When they buried the boy, Sayamma fell unconscious and it took more than an hour for her to regain consciousness. It had been a great shock to her. She cursed God for snatching her son from her, and kept fiddling with the dead child's toys even as she wept.

When Narsamma and Baliah returned to Nizamabad, the two sons and the daughter-in-law from Secunderabad came to stay with them for a few days to provide consolation and support.

Narsimlu, Anjiah and Sathiah were in class six, five and four respectively when Baliah seriously thought about shifting to Secunderabad where he could give his children a better and continuous education.

Sathiah Speaks

I was in class four when I started going to school on my own. Prior to this, it was my sister Bachamma who helped me cross the tracks to reach my school, which was located beyond a large open ground on the other side. It was a vast and sprawling field, and we used to play football there, taking care not to be seen by my father if he was on duty in the evening. My father had the notion that children who took too much interest in games and play would not study well, and every evening he would insist that we read. We were never allowed to play when he was around. If he found us playing, he would beat us and ask our sister to keep a watch on us.

The bungalows of the officers were on one side of the ground. While playing, I would often see my friend Ram Murthy standing at the gate of his bungalow; he was the son of the permanent way inspector (PWI), a Class I railway officer. He was a privileged boy, always accompanied by a gangman to school. Since they were Brahmins, his father did not allow him to play with untouchable boys like me. But Ram Murthy was my best friend. In the classroom, we sat next to each other and didn't think much of touching each other; he would even let me use the things he brought from his house. Caste and untouchability did not matter in our friendship: we were tender in age and innocent of this evil practice. However, in the presence of the gangman escorting him, he would pretend that he never touched me.

One hot afternoon, despite my resistance, Ram Murthy forced me to come into his bungalow. His father was away on duty and his mother had gone out. We sat on a sofa; it was fascinating for me as I had never before sat on a cushioned sofa. I jumped up and down on it, playing with my friend.

'You dirty pig, you untouchable! Get off! How dare you sit by our babu?' It was the Brahmin cook roaring.

I was terribly afraid, and sprang up from the sofa, running out of the bungalow even as my friend pleaded with me, asking me not to leave. As I looked back from the gate, I heard my friend shouting at the man, 'Why did you yell at my friend?'

'He is an untouchable! Go and bathe or I shall tell your father!'

I saw my friend chasing him, and the servant running away from him, yelling, 'Don't touch me, Babu, you are polluted! Go and take a bath!'

I walked away from the bungalow, cursing myself and wondering why I was untouchable. I was very angry with the servant: how did I cause pollution? This was not the first time I had encountered such humiliation. This happened whenever caste Hindus were around us. To them we were untouchables and people to be insulted and discriminated against. Strangely enough, though, all through my life some of my best friends have been Brahmins, and my brothers have often teased me, calling me 'pantulu', an alternative word for Brahmin.

My father used the word 'Harijan' whenever somebody enquired about our caste. Though he was a proud man who was fiercely against subordination, he was never unhappy about this observance of untouchability. To him, being 'untouchable' was part of the social set-up, and he did not know much of the civil society outside of the railways.

※

I entered the house expecting my mother to ask me why I was so disturbed, but found my parents engaged in serious discussion. My father held a paper in his hand.

'Balraja, I have been transferred to the city,' he was saying.

The practice of using one's spouse's name to address him or her was unheard of at the time, and my parents called each other Balraja, referring to the name of their firstborn. This time, the transfer was to the city of Secunderabad and my father appeared pleased.

My mother was not as cheerful. There was deep concern in her voice as she expressed her fear that her husband's salary would be insufficient to raise the family in the city.

Father was annoyed; he was well aware that here, my mother and sister could supplement his income by working in the paddy fields, but in the city they would have to live on his salary alone. It was his strong desire to send us to study in a big school, however, and he tried to convince my mother: 'Balraja, we will adjust. We can skip a meal if required, but our children *have* to go to a big school. There is a railway school there, and we need not pay anything.'

'Do you think your salary will be sufficient even if we keep skipping meals? In the city, I shall not find any work through which to help our family,' said my mother.

'Balraj is there. He will be of help to us,' said my father.

My mother did not want to be a burden on my brother since he now had his own family. But Father was resolute, and she reluctantly agreed to move to the city.

We were very excited. Each time my father was transferred, we happily packed our luggage and had great fun as we moved to the new place; we also got to travel by train! This time, unlike on earlier occasions, my father was also happy. It was his dream that his children be educated in the city. None of us children had ever been to the city, except Narsimlu, who sometimes went to Secunderabad to deliver groceries. Upon his return, we, the younger ones, would gather around him to hear about the big city. He would have a different story each time – how he had seen a 'bus over a bus' (a double-decker bus), or a cinema theatre over a building – and we would listen, rapt with interest. Our desire to visit the city would grow whenever he described his adventures there.

We had packed our baggage and our father had brought our transfer certificates from our schools. Ram Murthy came running to me on the last day. We strongly felt our impending separation.

'Are you leaving, Satti?'

'Yes, my father has been transferred and we are going to Secunderabad.'

Ram Murthy looked around, as if to check that the gangman was not in the vicinity, quickly placed a pen he had hidden in his pocket in my hands and ran away. He did not turn back to look at me.

All of us had been attached to Nizamabad and the pain of leaving it diluted the excitement of moving to a big city. It was the final transfer for my father; destiny was leading us to seek new turns in our lives.

The passenger train was now steaming towards the Secunderabad railway station. It was a great surprise to all of us to see the number of tracks, the many trains and the numerous signals above and across the tracks. This was a fantastic sight for all of us children, except Narsimlu. There were two large, long platforms separated by a number of tracks, one for broad-gauge trains and the other for metre gauge. As we got off, my mother shouted to us to stay together while she counted all of us – she wanted to ensure that none of the seven children was missing. Balraj was running towards us through a crowd of people. I had never before seen such a big crowd; many people were heading with their luggage towards the foot overbridge. I too wanted to climb the bridge, but my brother dragged me on to walk in the other direction, leading us down the platform. He and my father were carrying big trunks on their heads, while my mother was holding Laxman, our youngest brother, in her arms.

We started walking across the many tracks, looking at the wires connecting the signals. Two cabins, 'A' and 'B', were built at a height a little way from the entrance of the station, and it was from here that signals were given for incoming and outgoing trains by a cabin man.

There were three railway colonies near the station. The one closest to the station was called Cement File. The other two, on either side of the tracks, were called Pilcher File and Rethi File. A busy road separated Cement File and Pilcher File, both of which were colonies that accommodated pointsmen and gangmen. The British gave the suffix 'File' to the colonies since the quarters were attached to each other in a long line and there were several rows of such quarters, one behind the other.

We started walking towards Pilcher File, where my eldest brother had quarters. Some women peeped through their doors while others watched curiously. Seven children walking behind three adults like a train of ducks and ducklings – certainly a scene to attract attention!

The quarters allotted to Balraj was small, consisting of one big room, a little space for cooking and a small veranda. It was not sufficient even for all of us to sit together at once. We ate our dinner in batches. My father looked at Balraj questioningly.

'Don't worry, Father. Here, big families live in sheds they build in front of their quarters. They use the wall of the quarters in front as the supporting wall and extend the shed right across the intervening space to their own quarters.'

He showed Father a few such quarters; he saw what Balraj meant, and asked him to get the material necessary to build such a shed the next day.

It was a summer evening in the year 1956, and we all slept in the open that night. It came as a surprise to me the next morning to look across the open ground and see flames in several places. I woke up Narsimlu to ask him what this was all about. He was irritable. 'Why must you spoil my sleep? They are hearths, meant for cooking,' he said, and pulling up his bedsheet, went back to sleep. I went close to one of them: it was really a hearth, a cylindrical metal sheet standing on three legs, with a sheet at the bottom to hold coal, and three solid metal loops on the top to support a vessel. The coal was set alight and left until the flames subsided and the coal glowed red-hot. Then the hearth would be taken, by means of soldered wires, into the houses for cooking.

My father and elder brothers worked busily the whole of that day, erecting a large shed in front of the quarters. This was to be our home for several years to come.

My father was now talking to some friends: people who had worked with him earlier. 'When do we get water?' he asked one of them as his eyes chanced upon the tap at the end of the line of quarters. Each line had its own tap, and since water was not available all the time, there would be a queue to collect water.

'At six in the morning,' replied his friend. 'But, Baliah, there's a rule in our lane. Tulsi Ram, who works in the train examiner department, uses the tap first; others can touch the tap only after he has filled his water.'

My father was curious. 'Why? Is it his property?'

'He is a wrestler. Moreover, he is a Brahmin and has imposed the rule.'

'That's sheer injustice. Let me see tomorrow,' said my father.

That night, he instructed us to be ready early next day to fetch water. In the morning, my elder brothers were at the tap with our vessels, while Father himself sat a little to the side. Soon enough, a huge man with a cross thread on his shoulder approached the tap. Kicking away the vessel that was placed under the tap, he roared, 'Who the hell placed that pot under the tap? You fellows forgot the rule not to touch the tap before I do!'

My father was fuming; his eyes had turned red. Picking up the vessel, he almost pounced on the man. 'Why did you kick my vessel? This is not your father's property; whoever comes first will use the tap first.'

'Are you new? Don't you know the rule?'

'I don't care about your rule. This is the property of the railways and whoever comes first has the right to take water first.'

The man looked carefully at my father, who had first beat his own right thigh and then his left arm – a sign of a challenge to a fight, thrown by one wrestler to another. He looked at the people who had gathered around, and not having the courage to fight my father, he quietly left the scene. It was a victory for the people living in the lane. They were jubilant that the imposed rule had been broken, and from that time, whoever came first got water from the tap first.

The next day, my father took us to the railway school in north Lallaguda. The high school section was housed in a big building and towards its right were large sheds accommodating the primary and middle school sections. There were big trees all around, and a compound wall surrounded the school. Dressed in his crisp uniform, my father saluted the headmaster as he entered the latter's room with all of us in tow. The headmaster smiled at us. Our admission was easy since it was mandatory to admit the children of employees who came on transfer. Narsimlu and Anjiah were admitted in the sixth standard, while I was taken into the fifth. There were two different media of instruction in the school, Telugu and English. We had to opt for Telugu since we had studied only in that medium till then.

The very first day, we were part of a big assembly. I had never seen such a large gathering of students in my life. All the students from standards one to ten were standing class-wise. I was standing at the end of the row of boys studying in class five, curiously watching everything. There were more than a thousand students in the ground at morning prayers. The chorus of the prayer, accompanied by the music played by the band, reverberated in the school. The headmaster, Mr M.K. Narsimiah, the same gentleman who had admitted Abbasayulu into the school, was standing on a platform from where he could keep an eye on all the students. In his inimitable style, he wore a suit and shining brown shoes, and stood erect. He held a cane in his hand and watched every student as he passed by him, detaining those who were untidy in their appearance, or had uncombed hair and grown nails. I trembled as I passed this scrutiny, thanking God that I was properly turned out. This was, of course, because of my sister Bachamma, who always checked everything before sending us to school. The headmaster was one of my ideals and I was as impressed by the individual attention he provided every student as with his trim and tidy personality. He was the one who made me aware of the importance of suitable dressing for the rest of my life.

The school had a cross section of students, children of railway employees from various categories, except Class I employees. In the Telugu section, a majority of students' fathers were khalasis or unskilled labourers in the railway workshops, while most of the students in the English-medium section were children of higher-rank employees. In class, all the students mixed freely with each other.

Since it was the beginning of the academic year, I had not missed classes, but was a stranger to everyone. I sat on the last bench with my hand firmly on my bag, which held all the books my father had bought the previous day. My voice was very feeble as I responded to the teacher's roll call.

'Are you a new entrant? Speak out loudly,' he shouted at me.

'Yes, sir,' I stood up, shivering.

The teacher looked at me. 'Arey! Prem Kumar, let him sit by your side,' he said, and I, shy and timid as ever, went to sit near Prem Kumar, who later became my friend. He was in fact the best friend I had through my school years. Unlike my brothers, I could never make the first move and make friends easily, though I was friendly with those who came to me.

After school, Abbasayulu took us all to the nearby suburban railway station, Tukaram Gate, from where we boarded a local train to Secunderabad.

Lakshmibai and Yadagiri, the two younger children, had been admitted to a nearby government primary school. Now there were six of us going to school.

That evening, I saw Father arranging all that we required for our studies in the shed. He was trying to provide us an atmosphere in which we would not be disturbed from our studies. He placed two large kerosene lanterns, one in each far corner, and two rope-knit wooden cots in the shed; some of us could sleep on the cots and some under them. We had strict instructions from him to go to bed at ten o' clock and get up at four. My father would sit with us while we read aloud in the morning, making anyone who felt drowsy wash his face with cold water and come back to his lessons. Getting up early was a practice that we imbibed at this time, and even today, decades later, if I sleep beyond six in the morning, I have the consciousness of having done something I shouldn't have.

Six months and more had passed since we came to the city, and we were now settling in nicely. My mother and sister-in-law would be very busy in the mornings, making dozens of jowar rotis for our breakfast, and large quantities of rice and dal for our lunch at school. My father wanted us to eat together at lunch and would not allow us to carry individual lunch boxes. Anjiah and I would take turns carrying the huge lunch carrier for the four of us. As we ran, carrier in one hand and school bag in the other, to get to the station in time for our train, others on the station would often chuckle with amusement. Anjiah and I would sometimes grumble about this, but the older ones, Abbasayulu and Narsimlu, were happy with this arrangement.

Father took our studies very seriously. In fact, he kept track of the progress each of us made in school and even met our teachers to enquire about our performance. He discouraged us from loafing around with friends, and so did Balraj, who, like him, was a strict disciplinarian. None of our friends dared visit when my father or brother was at home.

The other task I disliked intensely was carrying sorghum grain on my head to the flour mill at the Regimental Bazaar. In the old days, my mother would grind the flour herself, but in the city, we boys carried the grain to the flour mills and brought back the flour. Given the size of our family, it would be a considerable quantity of grain, and passers-by would make fun of us, enquiring whether we were taking our load to a hotel. On Sundays, Narsimlu, Anjiah and I washed and ironed our clothes. Narsimlu would supervise the work, distributing it between Anjiah and me. I would iron all the trousers while Anjiah took care of all the shirts.

On the way to school, I would find Abbasayulu talking to his friends and classmates in English. I would sit close to him, trying to pick up words. I would enjoy their conversation without understanding it. It was my strong desire to learn English and speak it as my brother did. I tried to read the hoardings, the writings on railway coaches, wherever I saw English written – and my brother would correct me whenever I went wrong in my reading. I still remember the legend on goods wagons: 'Not to be loose shunted'. I remember too how I betted with my friend, Kulkarni, regarding the spellings of words. Soon, I learnt to memorize spellings. Kulkarni was a Marathi Brahmin, the son of a clerk. He was one of my closest friends, and a friend for life. Apart from him and Prem Kumar, I had other friends too – Madan Kumar, Chalapati and Simham.

1957: It was the end of the academic year and our annual examinations had begun. Abbasayulu was taking the board examinations. I would watch him studying seriously as he prepared for the exams. He would study until one o'clock in the night, and my father would sit with him if he was not on night duty. This brother of mine believed in hard work. My father had great hopes that Abbasayulu would get through the exams and become eligible for a good job in the railways; his ambition was to see Abbasayulu become a stationmaster. Needless to say, Abbasayulu did very well in his board examinations. He was the first matriculate graduate in our family. My father was overjoyed; he invited his best friends over to celebrate the event.

'Baliah, your son will now soon become a stationmaster,' reflected one of them, as he sipped a drink.

'Our job is to give our children a good education, which will take care of the other things in life,' said my father, with a smile.

'Baliah, I cannot do that. I have already requested the foreman to take my son on as a khalasi,' said another man.

Turning to him, my father said, 'I have decided to send all my children to school and give them a good education. Even if I have to skip a meal, it's all right. But I won't have them not going to school.'

This conversation left a deep impression on my mind, and his determination in this regard made me very serious about my studies as I moved into the sixth class. I became more active and responsive in the classroom.

Abbasayulu was seventeen and had to wait another year before he could apply for a job in the railways. In the meantime, he began to take up odd jobs to help my father. In the rainy season, for instance, he would help him by going out to note the flow of water under railway bridges. Working with my father and doing odd jobs meant that he had to go to different places, sometimes even at night, and my mother was unhappy about this. But my father encouraged him and would quite often tell us how a man should feel happy living on his own earnings.

One afternoon – it was the seventh of the month, I recall, because as usual on his payday, Balraj had bought his favourite chand biscuits, the sweet biscuits shaped like the crescent moon – when I came home from school, I found my father in high spirits, but my mother strangely sad. Abbasayulu had got an appointment as signaller in the telecommunications department of the railways. This was the job one had to undertake before becoming a stationmaster; and my father was jubilant because his cherished desire – his son serving as a stationmaster in the railways – was now sure to be fulfilled. My mother was sad because her son had to go to Bhusaval for his training.

Since he was to become a Class III officer, my brother needed better quality clothes and shoes. My father took a loan from a cooperative credit society and arranged to have four sets of clothes stitched for my brother, and bought him a good pair of shoes; he also purchased for him the first leather suitcase our family ever owned, instead of giving him the usual trunk.

At this time, my grandfather came to visit us. He had come after a long time and was now quite old and slightly bent, and used a walking stick. Each time he came, we children would gather around him to hear his tales of ghosts – we all loved him. I enjoyed helping him fill tobacco in a leaf that he would then roll into a tiny, elongated funnel. He still used the chekumuki rai – a device that used coarse pebbles, a fibre of jute and an iron rod – to light it. After a few puffs, he would extinguish the little chutta, a beedi similar in size to a cigar, and put it in the folds of his turban to reuse later. I watched him looking contentedly at Abbasayulu, who was dressed in his new clothes and was just stepping out. 'Ramaswamy, look at my grandson! See how gracefully he walks, like a ladsahib!' he said, looking at my father.

'Yes, Father, my son looks like a master,' my father smiled. Both continued to gaze at my brother until he was out of sight.

Abbasayulu started his career as a signaller in the railways, and quickly moved up the ladder to become a stationmaster. Later, being more interested in an academic career, he gave up his job as a stationmaster to become a lecturer. My father was very upset about this since being a stationmaster was better in his estimation.

※

1957 was also the year in which the railways stopped issuing rations and also the supply of subsidized groceries to railway staff. The enormous expansion of the railways and the growth in the number of employees made it difficult for the institution to continue with this provision. The result was that the employees suffered a sudden, heavy blow, and the effect was felt in our family too. Most large families had to open credit accounts with the local banias, thereby becoming permanent debtors.

The beginning of the academic year was a tough time. Each year, I would hear my father telling my mother that he had to withdraw money from his Provident Fund to get us books. As scheduled caste students, we received scholarships, but the amounts were meagre, and hardly sufficient to get even a pair of uniforms for each of us. My father ensured that he never used this money for any other purpose save our schooling needs. This year, though, Balraj too had to take a loan to meet our requirements.

Memorizing was my forte, and I could easily learn any lesson, long or short, by heart. I was at this time, therefore, always at the top of the class academically. But I had rivals. My arch rival was Madan Kumar, with whom I often had a neck-to-neck competition for the first place. He was good at mathematics, always scoring hundred per cent marks, but my grades in the other subjects were better. This made me stand first most of the time. He was the envious type. Although the caste factor usually remained in the background, he and his friends would tease me, indirectly referring to my status in the caste hierarchy. When I entered the class, he would point to the wall and ask his friends whose it was, and they would say 'Maadi (ours)'. And what was it that they were referring to, he would then ask, to which they would reply 'Goda (wall)'. Then he would ask them to combine the words, which they would do, and then loudly shout 'Maadi-goda' – a man or boy from the Madiga caste. I would feel humiliated and insulted, but never countered it – I knew I had no support against this group.

It was around this time that I developed a friendship with my classmates Pandari, a good football player, Krishna, Baliah and some others. Our school was one of the best in games and sports and had good facilities for hockey and football. We were consistent winners at the inter-school level in these games. Kabbadi was another sport that we were enthusiastic about. Narsimlu was a good kabbadi player, and part of the team representing the school in the inter-school competitions. Mr Francis, our physical training (PT) teacher, was very committed and was a hard taskmaster. He was rugged and tough, and did not spare anyone when it came to the rules of the game and good behaviour while playing. Although good at studies, I was reluctant to participate in sports, as a result of which the PT teacher was not satisfied with me. He was strict and in his class, he would never allow anyone to sit idle – which meant that every PT class was a nightmare for me. He had a foul mouth at times, and ordinarily used words like 'Abe' and 'ra', rude forms of address, when talking to students. Yet he was good at heart, and most students liked him. He was the most popular teacher in the school after the headmaster.

He was very particular that students present themselves in the regulation blue shorts and sleeveless banian, and if he found any boy dressed differently, he had to run non-stop around the ground for the duration of the class. I had to face this ordeal once; I fell flat on the ground when I reached home, crying with pain. My mother applied some balm on my aching body, cursing my PT teacher all the while. We had blue shorts, made from my father's old trousers but no banians; but after this incident, my father immediately bought us some.

The very next day, our geography teacher was absent. Whenever any teacher was absent, it fell to the PT teacher to engage the class. He would not take children out to the grounds unless it was his own class, but would engage us in learning good etiquette, a favourite topic of his. It was an interesting class – as most of us in the Telugu section of the school were the children of lower-order railway employees, we were quite curious to know what etiquette was.

'How do you drink from a cup of tea at a party?' asked our PT teacher.

'Pour it in the saucer and gulp it down' came the reply, in chorus.

He laughed loudly. 'You silly fellows! That is not how you drink tea. The saucer is given as a mark of respect and you should not pour tea into the saucer and gulp it like a dog, making a lot of noise. That is bad manners. You should hold the saucer properly and sip the tea gently from the cup. That is good manners.' It was quite amusing. He also taught us about dress codes and how to sport a tie, and to tie single and double knots. Being Christian, he was aware of table manners and behaviour appropriate at buffets, etc., and enjoyed teaching us the same.

'Do you know dining table manners?' was his next question, though he was sure nobody knew them.

'We don't know, sir.' The reply was once again in chorus. Then he explained to us how to fold a serviette; how to use a knife and fork; when to use a spoon; and how to cut a piece of meat or bread with a knife and fork without making a noise at the table. He also described to us the various food items found at the table at parties, including soup. Summing up, he asked us, 'After finishing your food, how do you say that you need no more?'

'We simply shout that we don't want any more food, sir' was the reply. He smiled at us. 'Not that way. You should invert your spoon and fork, and that is the sign that you require no more food.'

This was how his classes would go when he had to substitute for another teacher. We never felt bored in his class. I, of course, was happier with him in the classroom than on the ground. On this particular day, he called out to me after the class: 'Arey, Satti, you are good in the class, and that's fine. But you must have a strong body too.'

I was silent, having nothing to say. I knew that even my looks betrayed my poor health: I was very lean, to the point that my family sometimes called me 'bakkodu', the lean one.

Then he said, 'From now on, practise running for half an hour, daily. I shall put you on the football team next year.'

'Yes, sir, I shall practise' was my short reply as I ran to the next class.

※

My grandfather was now living with us. We had a herd of goats whom my grandfather took out to graze; I joined him on Sundays and holidays. He would let them graze in the open Railway Recreation Club grounds. In those days, in fact, right into the early 1970s, it was an open area. A compound wall at least two to three miles long enclosed a small stadium with huge grounds. Next to this was an uninhabited hilly area known locally as 'Adda Gutta'. As children, we would climb up and play on the hillocks while our goats grazed and Grandfather shouted at us, asking us not to disappear. In a little over thirty years, there has been a great metamorphosis in the geography of Adda Gutta; it has turned from uninhabited land to a place with hundreds of large residences and well-laid roads.

In the evening, the goats would be tied in one corner of the shed and the lantern cleaned and filled with kerosene. If the ropes of the cots had come loose, my grandfather would tighten them. He and Laxman shared a cot while Narsimlu and Anjiah slept on the other. Yadagiri and I would slip under the cots to sleep. The rainy season was bad for us; heavy rain would keep us awake for most of the night, and the goats, being drenched, would keep moving around uneasily, making a lot of noise. The continuous sound of water trickling into the dishes placed under leaky spots would sometimes awaken us, and we would frequently have to get up to empty the dishes. There were also times when the ground was completely wet, and we sat on the cots through the night.

In those days, we would have our dinner together, sitting in a long row: in all, including my grandfather, we were thirteen people at dinner. It was indeed a big number. My mother and sister-in-law would serve the food from large vessels while we ate silently, making no noise: my father was against talking while eating. We ate jowar roti and dal with some curry most of the time; on Fridays, though, lamb meat would be cooked, and my mother would serve us carefully, ensuring that each of us got a few pieces. My father and my grandfather would each eat from a big brass bowl, which they held in their left hands while they ate. The rest of us ate from aluminium plates. This practice of eating together once a day at dinner continued after the joint family broke up into individual families; even today, all the branches of the family continue this tradition. Of course, each family now eats at a dining table with the choicest dishes. Nevertheless, remembering those days makes me feel good; we shared happily what little we had.

My father was fond of travelling and, during the summer of 1958, planned to take us to Rishikesh, a pilgrim town in north India. A friend of his had told him about this place and the Ganga River that ran through it, and he was keen that all of us visit it. My mother started preparing for the trip with the help of my sister-in-law and Bachamma. They made snacks enough to last us seven to ten days, and made puris and pickles to last three to four days. We would travel on free passes but without reservations on the trains – my father never made reservations when we travelled.

The day when we were to leave came, and the family stood at the Secunderabad railway station, waiting for the Dakshin Express to arrive. We had a lot of luggage, and each of us was entrusted with at least one bag. Balraj carried a heavy box on his head containing rice, dal, edible oil and other items that would be cooked during transit halts; my father carried a trunk that contained the clothes of all thirteen of us; and my sister-in-law carried a big box containing cooked rice, dal and curries for us to eat during the journey. We also carried some dry firewood wrapped in cloth; Narsimlu and Anjiah took turns carrying this. We were standing around the luggage, looking in the direction we expected the train to come from. Balraj was busy talking to his colleagues who had come to help us get into the general unreserved third-class coach. As the train halted, all of us found seats in the unreserved compartment with the help of my brother's colleagues. I remember arguing with Lakshmibai about who would sit by the window, and finally agreeing to share it with her.

In those days, third-class compartments were like long, narrow rooms, and were fitted with wooden benches facing each other. Small fans hung from the roof of the train, but these were hardly enough to provide relief in the overcrowded compartments. Most stations were connected only by a single set of tracks which meant that, in order to avoid collision, trains on opposite sides had to wait for each other to clear the station before they could enter it. There were only steam engines which discharged a great deal of smoke when the trains moved at a high speed. I enjoyed sitting on Father's lap as I looked out through the window and watched everything 'move' in the opposite direction, but got smoke and dust in my eyes many times. In the evening, we reached Nagpur where my father bought a basketful of oranges. My mother gave us some snack every few hours. After dinner, my father and Balraj took out the sheets from the box and spread them out on the floor of the train between the benches, and we slept on those.

Spending a day and a night on the train was a new experience for all of us; I enjoyed the swinging and the swaying of the train, and its sounds as it ran along at a high speed. The next morning, we were woken up early, as usual, and before the other passengers were up, we had washed and were fresh. When I travel by train now, I am reminded of my childhood travel and chuckle to myself. Even if I am in a first-class coach, I get up early in the morning and go to the toilet as early as possible, while the other passengers are still in deep slumber.

My mother and sister-in-law served us tamarind-rice for breakfast. Around midday, the train passed through mountain ranges – it was fascinating to see the train pass like a snake between the mountains. Sometimes, all of a sudden, there would be total darkness, and the train would suddenly sound different. The first time this happened, all of us younger children screamed. I held my father tight, and in a few seconds, we came back into the daylight.

'Father, why was it suddenly dark?' I asked. 'We were really afraid!' My father smiled at me, 'The train was passing through a tunnel.'

'What is a tunnel?' We all wanted to know, and my father explained it to us like a teacher. Taking an orange, he made a hole right through the middle, 'Look! Suppose this is a mountain. I've made a hole right through it, right? In the same way, a tunnel is made in a mountain and the train passes to the other side through it.' He went on, 'It is dark since sunlight cannot pass through the mountain.'

Even as he spoke, we passed through another tunnel, but this time we were not afraid.

We reached Delhi that evening. The platform in Delhi was big; my mother took care to see that we were all together. We went to a nearby choultry, a shelter house meant for the poor, with common bathrooms and a big dormitory to sleep in. Here too, we got up early in the morning, before anyone else did, and bathed. I was particularly happy because I could now wash off all the dust accumulated in my hair – I had sat at the window for much of the time. We had our breakfast, puris and chutney, and set out on foot to see the vast city of Delhi. The wide roads of Delhi took us by surprise, as did the variety of vehicles, including tongas or horse wagons on the road. We walked to Connaught Place, a shopping hub that had large buildings in those days too. My father arranged with a couple of tongawalas to take us round the city and we visited important places like the Lal Qila (Red Fort), Jantar Mantar, India Gate, Rashtrapati Bhawan, etc. We packed quite a few things into our day; after all, we had to catch a train to Rishikesh in the evening.

In the evening, we boarded the train, sitting in the general compartment again. It was thrilling to watch the train moving over the bridges as we crossed the wide rivers. My father even gave me a one paisa coin to throw into the Ganga: an offering to Goddess Ganga, whose waters could wash away one's sins. The next day, we reached Rishikesh – a mountainous locale with lots of trees all around and the Ganga flowing merrily by. We went straight to the ghat to wash ourselves in the river. The water was cold as ice, and we shivered as we washed. My father and Balraj went much deeper into the waters than the rest of us. We then changed into dry clothes and went to a temple to offer prayers. Having shared living space with caste Hindus, we had adopted their manners and therefore felt no difficulty accessing temples. Only after this did we go to a choultry and had our breakfast, after which we went to the Lakshman Jhoola, a wonderful footbridge across the river. While walking on the bridge, one could feel it vibrating, even swinging in the wind. My father told me that it was known as jhoola (the Hindi word for swing) since it swung as people walked across it; also, it was believed that one of the heroes of the Ramayana, Lakshmana, had built it, thence the name Lakshman Jhoola.

We started back on our long journey home within a few days. We had less luggage on the way back since the stocks of food had been considerably depleted. In fact, we hurried for fear of not having enough food left. We reached Secunderabad after a trip of ten to twelve days, a journey that had been as exhausting as it had been enjoyable. My mother was greatly relieved – all through, she had been anxious about the large family and was hard-pressed to keep all of us together, worrying even if one went to relieve oneself, but particularly when we had to change trains. She frequently took my father to task for taking us on such a long journey and made him promise not to take the family on such extended trips ever again. In retrospect, that trip seems amazing – I now wonder how my father managed such a large family, travelling for days together without any berth reservations on the trains!

The summer vacation got over and the schools reopened. Narsimlu, Anjiah and I progressed to the next class. For days after school began, my friends would gather around me as I told them about our trip and about the city of Delhi. Yadagiri and Lakshmibai now moved to the railway primary school at Secunderabad, and Laxman began attending the government school closer home. As usual, my father had to apply for a PF loan to pay for our schooling. This time, he agreed to let us have separate lunch boxes – I was delighted!

Narsimlu and Anjiah were mediocre students, sometimes falling below average. I, on the other hand, stood first in class, but as before, struggled with mathematics. There was no one at home to teach me the subject. As I could memorize things easily, at times I even learnt mathematics problems by heart, without really understanding them! I was good at English, though. Quite often, my classmates would ask me to write leave letters for them. Our English teacher, Mr Sitarama Shastry, was one of the best teachers we had, one who did not utter even a single Telugu word while teaching English. I enjoyed his class and tried to adopt his style when reading aloud at home. My father would sit by me sometimes, keenly listening to what I read. Mr Shastry influenced me very much and inspired me too. He dressed well, many a time wearing a suit and sporting a tie. Yet most of my classmates were not happy in his class, for they could hardly follow what he taught.

As I said, there was a difference between the standards of the Telugu and English medium students, and segregation by class and caste came almost involuntarily. Most students from the Telugu medium would not qualify for the matriculation examination – a fact recognized even by the teachers – and most of them joined the railway workshop as unskilled workers. As children of railway employees, they could easily do so; access to these jobs was almost taken for granted – a khalasi's son could easily become one, just like his father. Often, their parents also wished for the same, since this brought in some money – sometimes they even withdrew their children from school for this reason. Like their parents,

these young people were also married early and had children early. My
father was against withdrawing children from school, and I often saw
him rebuking his colleagues for not ensuring that their children have a
better future. Very few students from the untouchable community (like
my brother) were in the English medium, and these students had a good
chance of securing better jobs after graduating through matriculation,
for English was desirable in government jobs.

Midway through the year, Abbasayulu completed his training at
Bhusaval and was posted in Bombay on probation. He came home on
leave to spend a week with us before going to Bombay – and brought
something for each of us. I found a great change in my brother, and in
the attitude of everyone around towards him: everyone paid him great
attention, the first man in our family to become an officer. So what if it
was at the bottom of the officers' hierarchy? Later, of course, my uncle
Yelliah too would become an officer, but at this time, and at this young
age, Abbasayulu was an officer! My grandfather was particularly happy,
and as he looked at the new set of clothes my brother had bought for
him, his eyes moistened involuntarily. For me, his favourite brother,
Abbasayulu had brought a beautiful pen that I preserved until I became
a graduate. He narrated to us his experiences as a trainee. He had
enjoyed the training and described everything in detail: what it was like
to sit with other trainees at a common dining table and eat – he even
described the food! He told us how each of them had his own cot and
a neat bed, and how most of them got up late in the morning and had
to hurry for breakfast. My brother was different because the habit of
getting up at four o'clock in the morning was ingrained in him. I asked
him unending questions about his experiences. Two evenings later, my
brother took me to the Minerva, where the film *Jis Desh Mein Ganga
Behti Hai* was showing, and even bought me snacks during the interval,
a treat I greatly enjoyed.

The week passed soon, and Abbasayulu set out for Bombay. A crowd had gathered at the station: apart from our own family, my father's and Balraj's friends and others from our community had come to bid him farewell too. My mother was crying silently. Her eyes were red and swollen; my brother tried to console her. We were sad that he had to go so far away. Abbasayulu waved to us as the train began to move and I wept inwardly as it disappeared from view; there was silence as we walked home.

It so happened that both my mother and sister-in-law were with child at this time. This was common in those times, mother-in-law and daughter-in-law bearing children at the same time. My mother gave birth to a girl and my sister-in-law to a boy. It was my mother's last issue. So now we had another little sister, a very cute, beautiful girl, almost a doll, whom we named Shama. Balraj's son was named Krishna Rao.

My sister-in-law bore other children later; she and Balraj would have a big family of their own, with seven children, the last two being twin boys.

It was during this year at school that I was selected by Mr Francis to be the goalkeeper of the football team: though lean, I had good reflexes. Abbasayulu, always unhappy with my bony structure, had, during his visit, managed to convince my father about the importance of games in a student's life. Now, we had his approval to participate in co-curricular activities.

Our football ground was on the other side of the railway tracks, and we had to walk across a stretch of open ground and cross the tracks to reach it. I started playing the game every day, practising regularly. A month before the inter-school competitions were to begin, we began to practise vigorously, playing each day for at least an hour after school.

This meant that we three brothers now no longer went home together but returned as our school and practice timings allowed. After a practice session, our teacher would offer us bananas or biscuits and spend time with us explaining the techniques of play. The league matches were soon announced; the strongest teams were those from St Patrick's School, St Mary's School and SPG School. Our teacher knew the strengths and weaknesses of the various teams, and coached us about the best way to defeat each. Practice time went up from one hour to two. One day, he took me aside and offering me some walnuts, said: 'Satti, you are a goalkeeper and the team's win depends much on you.'

In my enthusiasm, I would jump even to the corners of the goalposts to grab the ball. I was the best goalkeeper in the school, and popular because of this, but did not pay much attention to my injuries during play. This made my teacher a little worried about me, which is why he called me aside. 'Sir, I will make every effort and perform my best.'

He was satisfied with my response.

For the upcoming matches, we were given T-shirts, shorts and sports shoes. The first match was with St Patrick's School. The evening before the match, Mr Francis was tense during training. He was firm that no one should attempt to take the ball forward alone and that it should move on by being passed from one person to the other. He instructed me again on how to grab the ball from a player attempting a goal. After the session, we sat on the ground in a circle as he addressed us: 'Boys, it's time for you to give your best and make the school proud of you.'

'Yes, sir! We will defeat St Patrick's,' was our reply, in one voice.

'Yes, that should be the spirit. If you win, I shall treat you to biryani at the Alfa Hotel; and if you lose, *gudda bokkal iragodtha*, I shall break the bones of your backsides,' he said, smiling at us.

Now we not only wanted to win for the sake of winning, but also to be able to visit Alfa Hotel and have its famed biryani!

The match started promptly at two the next day at the Barton School grounds. Mr Francis gave us last-minute instructions and patting my back, said, 'Satti, the outcome of the game depends on you. Good luck!'

'We will win, sir,' I said, bowing my head respectfully.

It was a neck-to-neck match; the teams drew at two goals each. The referee then asked each team to shoot three penalty goals. I stood at the goal, ready for the ball, fully alert. I looked at the ball and the player who was to kick the ball: he was a good player, holding a backer position. He gauged the gap through which to get the ball into the goalpost. As he kicked the ball, I leapt to the right and held on tightly to the ball although I fell. Loud cheers resounded behind me. I had scraped my elbow and it was bleeding. Mr Francis ran to me with a first-aid box. I was so excited that I did not care about the bleeding. The next person to kick was from our side: Pandari was an excellent player and as everyone looked on, he swiftly hit a goal from the left corner. There was applause from our boys, who were now jumping and dancing.

Another player from the other team came forward to take the next shot. Their PT teacher was giving him serious instructions. My elbow was paining, but I was determined to 'do or die', as preached by our PT teacher. This time, although the player was looking at the right corner, he hit the ball straight into the centre, and I was able to catch it without much effort. Now, the score was one–nil and it was our turn to shoot. Pandari took position and hit a goal. We had won! Our boys danced on the ground and sang victory songs. My teacher was so happy that he hugged me, and my friends held me up on their shoulders, shouting jubilantly.

In the evening, as promised, we were treated to biryani at Alfa Hotel. This was my first success in a game, excellence in an area different from academics. I was euphoric. When I reached home that evening, Balraj saw my injury and scolded me, and warned me not to play any more. Learning about this the next day, Mr Francis came home personally to try and convince my brother that I would become a great player in future and that he was not to worry about small injuries. I was really surprised at the level of his dedication to the game! That was the kind of commitment teachers in those days had.

That year, we won the inter-school football event. After this, I became quite well known in the school; even the headmaster called me to his room to congratulate me. It gave me great confidence. Even today, the scars on my elbows and knees remind me of those days and of my teacher.

It was close to the end of the academic year, and exams were in progress. As usual, my competition was with Madan Kumar, who challenged me saying that he would beat me and come first in class. I was serious when it came to studies, but had to assist in household tasks as well. One task I did was to carry his dinner to my eldest brother when he was on duty between sixteen to zero hours – the last shift. When Balraj was on this shift, at about eight in the night, I would carry a box of food across the rail tracks to a cabin where I would leave the box for him. Anxious about the challenge Madan Kumar had thrown me, I chose a section of a lesson before I left the house and kept repeating it in my mind as I walked towards the cabin. So engrossed was I in repeating my lesson as I walked along a rail track that I did not hear a train approaching from behind. It could have been disastrous if all of a sudden a pointsman had not pulled me out of the way. I could have lost my life! The man slapped me out of my absorption. Then onwards, I did not dare repeat lessons in my mind while carrying food to my brother!

The school examinations got over, and I stood first once again. However, I was still lagging far behind Madan Kumar in mathematics. The report cards were given out. As I walked home from school that evening, my school bag on my shoulder, a gangman, the father of one of my classmates, called me, 'Arey, Sathiah, let me see your progress report!'

I handed it to him. He looked at it and appeared very unhappy. He said, 'Don't you study well? You haven't got even a single red mark, and my son says red marks indicate good marks. He always has red marks all over.'

I was amused at this and laughed, 'A red mark means that you have failed in that subject.'

The realization struck the gangman that his son had been fooling him, and he was extremely angry. I walked away as he stood there, waiting for his son.

My father planned a long trip again: this vacation, he would not take the whole family but only Narsimlu, Anjiah and me to Bombay, where Abbasayulu worked. We were very excited about the trip. My mother and sister-in-law prepared snacks in large quantities for my brother, whom we had not seen for nearly a year. He worked as a signaller at the Victoria Terminus – perhaps the biggest station in the Indian Railways at the time.

We arrived at Bombay station; Abbasayulu was there to receive us. Oh! What a big station it was! I looked all around even as my brother hugged me. Abbasayulu, being an officer, lived in a small hotel in Parel with a colleague. I was twelve, and was in one of the biggest cities of our country; I was thrilled to bits! There were huge buildings all along the way to the hotel and vehicles moved in three rows on the road. There were trams on rails and people moved busily on the footpaths. The hotel where Abbasayulu put up was small, but we were staying in one for the first time in our lives, and it offered us a completely new experience. They gave us extra 'beds': cushioned mattresses! I kept jumping on them with excitement. The next day, my brother's friend took us round the city, to Juhu Beach, Chowpatty and the Gateway of India. We were delighted to see the Arabian Sea. The ocean stretched till it touched the sky – it was fabulous! We went for a ride on a steamboat. In the evening, we had dinner at the hotel, where a smiling, courteous boy served us: I still remember that he was called Sakha Ram.

We stayed in Bombay just for a couple of days: my father knew it would be very expensive for Abbasayulu otherwise. My brother took us to the railway station. As he waved to us, the train steamed out of the platform, screeching. It had been a wonderful experience. My father was thoughtful: Abbasayulu's probation in Bombay was almost over, and he was expecting a transfer, but in the Bombay Division. That would still keep him far away; my father began to give serious thought to how he could be moved to the Secunderabad Division.

I was in the eighth class when we moved into new quarters in Rifle Range, where the railway tracks ran over forty feet above the surrounding areas. There were three different kinds of quarters – with one bedroom, two bedrooms and three bedrooms – and even the smallest had a bathroom and lavatory attached. This innovation in design was in itself novel to us. These quarters were allotted to employees based on the categories they worked in. This house was bigger than the earlier one, but still not sufficient for all of us. However, it was located in a corner, and there was enough open space to build a shed. This was the quarters where we lived for a long time, until after the three of us completed our matriculation and PUC (pre-university course, the precursor to today's intermediate or +2 level) education.

The quarters were much closer to our school and we began to go to school on foot. Earlier, we used to take a local train, and in summers particularly, when school began early, we would take a special train known as the 'workman'. This was a blue train that shunted between Secunderabad and Lallaguda each morning at seven, carrying all the employees who worked in the railway workshop adjacent to our football ground. I practised football regularly, but concentrated on studies as well. As usual, my father spent everything he earned either on our studies or on the food, and life became very tough for both him and Balraj. He also had to sell several of the goats to meet our expenses. Many of my father's friends advised him to stop Narsimlu's and Anjiah's schooling and send them to work in the workshop as casual labourers. But my father was firm that they should study, even though there were times when we had to live on jowar roti and chilli paste. We never grumbled: there really wasn't much we could do about it, anyway.

Around this time, the railways were laying new tracks alongside the existing ones and was dumping tons of coal ash day and night to make a large bed for the new track. This ash contained some coal that was not fully burnt. Given the quantities of coal ash being dumped, the amount of unused coal in it was significant. Women and children from the railway quarters would sift through the ash and collect this coal in baskets and sell it to the nearby lime kilns at three annas a basket. There were several of these kilns in a nearby locality. We – four brothers, two sisters, and sometimes a sister-in-law – also collected coal this way and carried the baskets on our heads and walked about a mile to Padma Rao Nagar to sell the coal. In this way, each of us would fetch more than a rupee every day, a large sum by the standards of the time. This money made a difference to the family funds. It remains one of the most unpleasant jobs I have ever done. Narsimlu, though, was happy to do it, for he never gave the whole amount at home but hid away some for himself. With this money, he would go to the movies and encourage us to do so too, specially my sister-in-law. She, a mild person, always nodded her head in reply. Sometimes each of us kept a paisa with us for every basket sold.

This coal collection was a great nuisance for the railways, though, and it began to take measures to arrest the menace. There began frequent raids on people sifting through the ash: the lathi-wielding Railway Police Force (RPF) personnel would pounce upon them, seize their baskets and beat them. Coal collection thus became difficult, and soon stopped.

※

It was during this time that Bachamma got married to Rajiah, a worker in a textile mill. Rajiah was a good wrestler and well known in the Ranigunj area of Secunderabad for his prowess. Rajiah's people had not been transparent during the pre-wedding talks: they made us understand that they lived in a big house, but we later found out that they occupied only a small portion of the large house. My parents were very unhappy when they came to know this. They had made Bachamma discontinue school after sixth standard: my mother had always discouraged her from going to school, saying it was not worth sending a girl to school. My father bitterly regretted that decision now; it might have helped him find a better match for her. The truth is that in our family, as in most others in those days, including higher-caste families, girls' education was not considered important, a thought that my father consoled himself with.

It was also around this time that Abbasayulu was transferred from Bombay to Jalna, and he now began to visit us once a month.

We always had a stream of visitors. My brother's quarters was small, yet, many relatives either from my father's or mother's side would come visiting and stay a few days. This made it difficult for us to study, especially during winter and the rainy season, when everyone was cramped into the small rooms. As it was, my brother had converted the kitchen into a bedroom, and a small portion of the veranda into the kitchen. To reach the washroom in the middle of the night, one had to walk over sleeping people, ensuring that one did not step on them. To this crowd were added my maternal uncle Ramiah and his wife, who came to live with us. They were accommodated in the veranda. I wonder now how my father and Balraj managed the continuous flow of relatives in such a small house, and that too on salaries that hardly met our own needs!

Despite the financial problems, my father was in the habit of smoking local cigars and drinking in the evening. One of us, often I, would go to the arrack shop to get a pint of Dubara and one of Rasi. Balraj was against sending children to the arrack shop, but he did not dare tell my father this; instead, he kept watch to see that all was well whenever we were on these errands.

It was nearing the end of the academic year. We would be examined on everything taught over the last three years. We had some very good teachers: Mr Sarangapani, who taught us history and geography, was one of the best. He never looked into a textbook in the classroom, but taught us whatever we needed to know. His lucid explanation and narration made me want to study further. I wondered how he could remember the dates – I found those difficult to memorize. But I remembered his lessons as if they had been told as stories, and history was one of the subjects in which I scored well.

Another teacher was Mr Parabrahma Shastry, who taught us Telugu. His voice was melodious and his recitation of poems simply marvellous. Everyone enjoyed it, and listened to him in pin-drop silence. Madan Kumar and I were his favourite students, and he encouraged us to recite poems ourselves – he would make us recite at least one in each class. He once challenged us to memorize a lesson titled 'Khandikya Keshi Dwijulu' in three days. It was rather long, running into eight or nine pages, and tough, containing a number of Sanskrit words, but Madan and I accepted the challenge. I recited it without a flaw on the third day and received much applause from my teacher and friends. Madan wasn't asked to recite at all, since I had already recited it.

Mr Shastry was a Brahmin, and he knew that I was an untouchable; but he took great interest in me and often said that I was an exceptional student. It was his influence that turned me into a vegetarian, making me lean towards learning more of the Hindu Sanskritized culture. I began to visit a nearby Ganesh temple to hear the discourses, mostly

Harikathas, or stories of Lord Hari, daily. These included many stories drawn from the Ramayana and the Mahabharata, and influenced me a good deal. I was rather spiritual at that age and my brothers and father would tease me, calling me 'pantulu'.

The annual exams were over. This time, my father decided that we boys would visit Rameshwaram, a pilgrim centre in the southernmost part of the country, with him. It was a long journey and I stayed close to my father throughout. We reached the Madras station after travelling a whole day and a night. After a bath and breakfast, we set out on foot to the Egmore railway station, from where we had to catch a metre gauge train to take us to Rameshwaram. The people of this region spoke Tamil, but we were familiar with the language since many railway employees in Secunderabad were Tamilians. We could follow what our co-passengers were saying but couldn't communicate with them as we could not speak the language. I read out the names of the railway stations as we crossed them; my father was proud of my ability to read. He bought idly and sambar for us in the train: it was the first time that my brothers and I had eaten these foods and we all enjoyed the idlis. In 1958, idlis and sambar were new to Hyderabad and the Telangana area; there, what we had were Irani hotels offering tea, bread and samosas. People sat in these little hotels chatting for hours together and sometimes sipping ponas. Pona is a tea that has more milk or cream than usual. 'One-by-two chai' (a single cup of tea divided into two cups and shared by two people) was popular in those days. Now, most of these Irani hotels have given way to eateries or other establishments and we do not find pona even in the few remaining ones.

The metre-gauge train was not as fast as the broad-gauge one, and it stopped suddenly: it was an amazing sight that I saw through the window! Nothing but water as far as I could see! We were at the edge of an unending sea. I was suddenly frightened, and held my father tight, 'What is this, Father? Are we drowning?' My father smiled at me and holding me close, said, 'Do not worry, it is an ocean, the Indian Ocean.'

It was then that I remembered that my history teacher had showed us a map of India and pointed out the Indian Ocean towards the south of the country. I found out then that this place was Pambam, a railway station where the train stopped before getting on to a long bridge across a stretch of the ocean. This bridge would open vertically from the middle to give way to ships that had to pass through: a marvellous feat of engineering undertaken by the British. The train would run on the bridge very slowly, as slow as a man walking. As we chugged across the bridge, I closed my eyes and held Father's hand tight; I had the feeling that I might fall into the serene waters any moment. I heaved a sigh of relief when the train was on firm ground again. We finally reached Rameshwaram, a place reputed to be the site where Rama worshipped Lord Siva before he waged war against Ravana. My father told me that Rama, with the help of an army of monkeys, had built a bridge right across the ocean in order to reach Lanka, where he battled with and killed Ravana. I remembered this story which I had heard once at a Harikatha.

The temple at Rameshwaram was huge. I had never seen one as large as this before. It had a long corridor through which we passed before reaching the sanctum sanctorum. A priest took us to several wells from where we could draw water to sprinkle on our heads (symbolic of a purifying wash), and asked us to worship each one. A priest standing near the deity poured a liquid into my hands, and I touched this to my eyes and gulped it down, thinking it to be an oblation. It was extremely bitter, and I realized that it was sandalwood paste that I had to rub on my cheeks – that is what everyone was doing. My brothers looked around and did the same, and we laughed about our ignorance. We noticed a guide showing other pilgrims some red streaks: legend had it that these were the bloodstains of Hanuman, whose tail was severed when he tried to uproot a Sivalingam installed there earlier.

It had been a long journey and we were so tired that we slept early that night. The next day, we began our way back home. We arrived home to tragedy; we had lost Shama, our infant sister, to chickenpox. Mother broke down upon seeing us; my father began to wail loudly too. All of us were shocked at losing the lovely little child. An elderly lady from the neighbourhood came to console us. My mother was berating my father for having left them, and he could not speak except to curse himself for doing so. We went to the ground where my sister was buried. My father fell on the little mound and wept. Balraj had to lift him bodily and take him away from the scene. We mourned Shama's death for ten days.

After the vacation, I moved to the ninth standard, and Narsimlu and Anjiah to the tenth. This time, my father had to apply for a cooperative credit society loan to get books and other school requirements for us. We too made every effort to do our best, lest we have to work as khalasis.

Abbasayulu had now become an assistant stationmaster in the Bombay Division. My father celebrated the event by inviting all our close relatives to a feast. From Secunderabad to Kazipet, people of our community were talking of my father who, despite being a Class IV employee, was educating his children and now had an assistant stationmaster for a son. My grandfather was the happiest. He felt proud that it was he who had taken the first step to make all this possible. On his monthly visits, Abbasayulu would ask me about my studies, and I would be happy and eager to spend time with him. Narsimlu and Anjiah avoided him for exactly the same reason – they did not want to tell him how they were faring at school!

'Sir, may I avoid the inter-school games this time?' I was hesitant even as I asked this question of Mr Francis.

He replied in all seriousness, 'Satti, no, you cannot do that. We are on a winning streak just now.'

'But I must concentrate on my studies; I am in my pre-final year.'

'This season will be your final one and I will not ask you to participate in your final year.' He looked worried, and convinced me that I had to play to uphold the name of the school. He explained how I was the best goalkeeper the school had and how difficult it would be to replace me at such short notice. I had great respect for him: apart from his skill as a teacher, he took great care of me. Knowing my background, he often offered me nutrient-rich snacks so that I could develop my stamina. I did not want to refuse him.

At this time, I also won a prize: I received a dictionary for winning an inter-class essay writing competition in English. It was very precious to me and I preserved it until my postgraduation. Our English teacher, Sitarama Shastry, paid me a lot of attention as I was the only person who dared to say a few words in English though I was studying in the Telugu medium. He encouraged me to write, and inspired me to learn further. Once, during his lesson, a peon from the headmaster's office peeped into our class, and called, 'Who is Sathiah?'

I stood up.

He said, 'The headmaster would like to see you.'

As I left the class with my teacher's permission, I was afraid, and wondered why I had been called.

The headmaster's room was generally out of bounds for students, and I was entering it for the first time. It was a large hall, and on the wall behind his seat hung a portrait of Mahatma Gandhi. A showcase along the same wall held many trophies, all won by the students. The headmaster was sitting majestically in his chair.

'May I come in, sir?' My voice was feeble.

'Yes, come in, Sathiah.' It was a firm, deep voice.

I stood quietly before him, with folded hands.

'Congratulations, child, you won the football match.' He was referring to last year's match.

'Thank you, sir; we won it together.'

'But you were the boy behind the team's efforts to save the goals.'

I smiled and kept silent.

'Look, Sathiah, you are also good at your lessons. You may become a big man in the future. But your name will come in the way of your progress. I advise you to change your name to Satyanarayana.'

'Sir ...' I did not know what to say.

'I shall inform your father and make the change.'

I was happy that my headmaster was showing such concern for me, and in something as personal as a name. He had always taken a keen interest in his pupils. Sometimes, with the parents' approval, he changed the names of students if, in terms of caste, it seemed to represent something contemptible. In my case, the suffix '-iah' gave away my caste. One of my classmates was called Simham (meaning lion), and his name was changed to Narasimham, a Hindu God's name. The headmaster did this while sending our names to the Board of Secondary Schools. I wonder how many heads today look into minute aspects of individual students and take care to make necessary changes. He became an ideal for me to follow in life.

It was in the ninth standard, then, that I became Satyanarayana.

It was a hot summer. Narsimlu and Anjiah wrote their exams in their public exam centre, Mahboob College, one of the oldest schools in Secunderabad. There was some discussion about whether my brothers should seek jobs in the workshop. My father was strongly against it and insisted that my brothers continue their education. He had also been making efforts to arrange for Abbasayulu's transfer to the Secunderabad Division, and a mutual transfer finally came through: a man from the Marathwada area agreed to the exchange of positions and my brother was transferred to Godamgura, a small station close by.

'Baliah, I've just seen a girl who would be a good match for Abbasayulu,' said Ramiah, my father's friend, to him one day.

Father was immediately interested – he was already searching for a girl for my brother. 'Whose daughter is she?'

I was reading in a corner of the veranda they were sitting in, and could not help overhearing the conversation.

'She is muqaddam Narsiah's daughter; he works in Kazipet.' He continued, 'She is fair and good-looking, and goes to school.'

'How many children does Narsiah have?'

'Two sons and a daughter. The sons are older and one of them works in TXR; the other is a gangman. It is an affluent family.'

'Let me discuss this with Balraj and I shall let you know,' my father concluded, an eye suddenly on me, looking to see if I was actually studying.

The matriculation results were to be announced in the papers. My father bought a newspaper and sat in the veranda checking the results, with Balraj looking on. Narsimlu and Anjiah waited nervously inside, almost hiding from Father. The whole family waited anxiously as he looked through the first and second division columns, but could not find their numbers. Narsimlu and Anjiah were tense as he called me to look again. Going through the list all over again, I found their numbers in the third division. Father and Balraj were angry and upset, and it made my brothers very hesitant to come out and face them. Finally, my mother came to their rescue and my father and Balraj calmed down with her intervention.

Two more matriculate graduates had been added to the Yelukati family. It had been my father's mission to educate his children, and this was actually a mark of great success. The good thing was that the low marks did not deter my father from pushing Narsimlu and Anjiah from pursuing higher studies. Abbasayulu had satisfied one ambition of his by becoming a stationmaster, but now, with the help of his two elder sons' earnings, he wanted his other sons to aim higher. And the wonderful thing was that our two older brothers were equally committed to that goal.

There was a marked change in our family's economic condition as well, reflected in our lifestyle. Now our staple food consisted of wheat, rice and dal; from jowar roti we had switched to chapattis made of wheat flour. Some of the earthen pots had been replaced by aluminium ware. We had started drinking tea in the mornings, with a little milk. We had other desires too – I craved for a radio, a wish that was fulfilled when Abbasayulu got married and his father-in-law gifted us one.

Abbasayulu would visit once a month and he generally came during the first week of every month. Coming home now, he was not satisfied with Narsimlu and Anjiah's results. However, he agreed with Father that they should do the pre-university course. He procured admission forms for the Secunderabad Arts and Science College for them. Since the scheduled castes and tribes could avail of free education, they got admission easily. My father bought two sets of clothes for each of them, and they had trousers for the first time! They started attending classes, and would tell me new things about the college every day. I learnt that most of the students there were from the city, and came from well-to-do families. They had studied in the English medium and spoke only in English. In those days, the only medium of instruction in colleges was English. Having studied in the Telugu medium, Narsimlu and Anjiah found it difficult to cope, and were upset and unhappy.

Bandaru Mysiah was a local leader at Chilkalguda, the area where Abbasayulu had once lived. He was a municipal corporator and had a cement-and-brick house with a big hall, and encouraged needy Harijan boys to study in his house. He had three daughters and a son. We knew the family, and Abbasayulu had been friendly with his elder daughter Yadamma when they were neighbours; but when Balraj moved to Secunderabad, they lost touch. Mysiah too had been transferred to a remote place. One day, he turned up at our door. It was a pleasant surprise for my father. They sat in the veranda, exchanging pleasantries. My mother served tea.

'Boney, it appears you are looking for a bride for your son,' said Mysiah.

'Yes, it is time he should be married,' my father said.

'Boney, have you forgotten your promise?'

'What promise?' My father was surprised.

'You promised four years ago that you would make my daughter your daughter-in-law.'

My father tried to recall when he had made such a promise; of course, they had been good friends four years ago. Mysiah tried to jog Father's memory – the promise had been made when they were sitting over a drink.

My mother, listening from the inner room, called my father in and said in a low voice, 'You might have made such a promise. I know that when you drink with your friends, you lose control and talk as you want.'

My father did some serious thinking – could he have made such a commitment? Also, he had heard that Abbasayulu was secretly meeting Mysiah's daughter. Perhaps it would be better for everyone if Abbasayulu married Yadamma.

'Okay, Mysiah, it seems my son likes the girl too.'

Mysiah smiled; he touched my father's feet and they hugged each other.

Abbasayulu's wedding had been fixed for the summer. He was happy with the idea of marrying Yadamma, whom he met frequently while in Godamgura. Mysiah had known of it, and they had his tacit encouragement.

My father and Balraj were busy with the preparations. Mysiah wanted his daughter's wedding to be a big event. He invited several political leaders, and many ground-level workers. A small function was held on the day the wedding date was fixed. After the lunch, close relatives from both sides gathered to discuss what the bride's parents would give to the groom and vice versa. This dialogue is known as mata-muchchata.

'I shall give your daughter two tolas of gold, silver anklets, a silk sari and other things.' My father's voice was firm.

'Anna, what do you propose to give my son?' asked my mother in a low voice.

'Sister, I shall give him a half-tola gold ring, kitchenware, a cot, a bicycle and other things,' said Mysiah. I sat in a corner, listening to people expressing their opinions. Ultimately, the proposals were mutually agreed upon.

It was May. We were seeing a wedding performed in a banquet hall for the first time – that too my own brother's! There were a large number of invitees. There was a band too, unlike the beating of drums that was the norm in our community. My brother's Brahmin friends made fun of the baindlaina performing the ceremony because of his non-Brahminical accent and since he only knew the 'Shuklambara' mantra. After the wedding, Yadamma came to our house in Rifle Range. She was henceforth called Krishnaveni. My brother had to wait for some time before he could take her with him to Makudi, the station where he was now posted, for he still did not have proper quarters.

For over fifteen years (since 1960), my family went through a very difficult time. In addition to financial problems, my mother's health was indifferent. She also went into a trance sometimes, and some believed that Goddess Durga, who was much revered in my eldest sister-in-law's house, had come to us after the eldest sister-in-law got married. Father took Mother to a holy man in a nearby locality and she went into a trance in his presence. The holy man made her untie her hair and applied ash on her forehead. She started screaming loudly, taking the names of gods and goddesses, and suddenly sat upright and then got into the padmasana, remaining in a trance all the while. Placing her palms on her knees, she began to rotate her body from the hips. I was terribly afraid and could hear the people sitting around us whispering: 'The goddess is entering her body.'

The holy man sat with folded hands asked her who she was.

'Don't you know? I am Goddess Durga.'

He placed burning camphor in my mother's palm; she circled her palm around the portraits of the gods and threw the camphor aside, clearly not in any pain. I wept as my mother then fell unconscious. Father lifted her up; she immediately regained consciousness: it was as if she had just woken up from sleep. There was a deep burn in her palm, and she now inquired how that had happened.

This incident had a great impact on my family. Hitherto, we observed no regular rituals or worship except during festivals. Now, my mother would frequently go into a trance, her hair loose, holding a ball of ash in her hand and reciting the names of all the gods and goddesses in a high-pitched voice. Father and Balraj would sit in front of her with great devotion and reverence and Father would ask, 'I seek your shelter, Mother. Why have you come?' My mother, her body rotating even as she sat with half-closed eyes, making loud hiccup-like sounds, would reply, 'I came to bless the children.'

My younger sister would shout for us, calling us all, and we would prostrate ourselves before our mother, after which she would apply ash on our foreheads. This became a weekly ritual in our family for a long time.

※

It seemed strange to me when people called me Satyanarayana. At home, I began to be called Satyam.

My school had a new building in southern Lallaguda – a beautiful new building that today houses the IRIEST hostel. As senior students of the school, the ones about to appear for the public exam, we were privileged above others. Each teacher was doing his best to finish his assigned portion of the syllabus as soon as possible, so that we could begin a revision of the key concepts. Mr Francis too kept his word and did not involve me further in sports; on the contrary, he regularly inquired after my studies. There was great competition among us, particularly between Madan Kumar, Prem Kumar, Shahabuddin and me. We were in the grip of exam fear: I gave up all other activities, prepared a schedule for the revision of the eighth and ninth standard syllabuses and started studying. I spent every waking moment going over lessons from the three-year syllabus. It had become a mission for me, a great competition, and I would not reveal my strategy to my competitors, always telling them that I had not yet seriously started preparing. It was a tough course, matriculation, and achieving a first class was a great task in those days of severe marking of scripts.

Exams would soon be upon us again: my father concentrated on my younger brothers now, but he still did not allow us to study beyond ten in the night and continued to ensure that we got up at four o' clock in the morning to study. The truth is that my father's efforts were greater than our own at the time of our exams; he would apply for leave for fifteen days and watch over us.

Narsimlu and Anjiah were anxious. They had purchased study guides since it was impossible for them to go through the textbooks, which were in English and slowed down their rate of learning. When the medium of instruction had changed, they had suddenly been pushed into an alien world. They did not dare express this to my father or Balraj, but Abbasayulu knew their position. Nevertheless, they were putting great effort into trying to memorize their lessons. In the early hours, we would all read aloud; the strange thing was that no one was disturbed by the others. Now, I wonder how the five of us sat in a row under the kerosene lamps and read aloud for the exams: just a few years ago, each of my four daughters needed a separate room for their studies!

Electricity came to the railway colonies in the early months of 1961 – the streets too were lit up. It was fascinating! The move from kerosene lamp to electric bulb was a great experience. I was literally reading in a flood of light. Sometimes I enjoyed myself reading under a streetlight, but this was only when my father was not at home. People soon abandoned kerosene lanterns.

Like my brothers before me, I had to write my public exams in the strange and unfamiliar environs of Mahboob College. All the teachers, particularly my headmaster, were optimistic about me, and confident that I would secure a first class. My headmaster had called me into his room and said, 'Look, Satti, next to your parents, your teachers would be most happy with your success. I have made the little change in your name in the hope that it will give you self-confidence. I am certain that one day you will become a great man. All the best.'

'Thank you, sir!' My eyes dampened with happiness, but I did not know if I would be able to meet his expectations, and therefore felt worried.

The first day in the exam hall, I felt nervous when I saw the serious atmosphere of the place – the teachers and invigilators were new to us. Nevertheless, as I started writing, I gained confidence. I did well in all subjects except mathematics in which, though I had attempted all the questions, I was not confident of getting good marks.

My elder brothers also wrote their PUC exams and did not seem very enthused about their prospects.

It was in the last week of May 1961 that the results of the matriculation exams were declared in the press. My father had brought a newspaper;

he was very anxious and called for me. Balraj took the paper from him and looked for my number several times in the first division column, but could not find it. In the meantime, some of my friends shouted from outside that I had passed in the second division. I was upset and did not believe it, and searched the paper repeatedly – but my passing with a second division did not change. I had missed the first division by eight marks: throughout my academic career, I was to remain a second division student. I was sad, and my father could not believe it either. But he was somewhat consoled when he came to know that no one from the school had passed with the first division that year.

It was a shock to all the teachers that the school had not produced even a single first class that year. I went to the school after three days, and the teacher I first met was Mr Sita Ramanadam. Looking at my marks in English, he said, 'Satyam, I am sure that there must be something wrong! You can never get thirty-five in English; the second paper, worth fifty marks, might have gone unvalued! Go for a revaluation.'

His firm faith gave me a little consolation. I had got a little more than sixty per cent in every subject except English, in which I was strong. It was some consolation that I had stood first in the school. My father had no regrets; he was happy that I had stood first in class. My teachers congratulated me, especially Mr Francis who was happy with my performance and advised me to take part in games during my higher education as well.

The PUC results were announced a week later: both Narsimlu and Anjiah had been detained. Some of our relatives were of the opinion that they should find jobs. My father was dejected but was against discontinuing their education. Balraj too thought that they should be given a chance for improvement. Father sent word to Abbasayulu for his opinion. After going through their marks memos, Abbasayulu advised them to appear again for the subjects they had failed in: English and biology. Father was agreeable to this though this meant that they had to stay at home the whole year preparing to rewrite the exams. This was typical of Father: he encouraged us even when we did not fare well. He never believed in quitting; rather, he believed that we would learn from our failures. Had he believed otherwise, we could not have studied further, for lessons were really a struggle in college – we had little or no guidance, and the language in which we had studied at school was not helpful to us any more.

There was a complete change in the institutional atmosphere too, and we developed an inferiority complex amongst the other students in college. We did not dare talk to the teachers or students, except for a few backbenchers who were of our social background. Teachers and students of the higher classes could easily identify us as Dalits and looked upon us with contempt. Our names appeared last even on the attendance register, indicative of our social status.

Like my brothers, I joined the Secunderabad College of Arts and Science. My father had two pairs of new clothes made for me, as he had done for my brothers. I was going to wear trousers for the very first time. A bus went from Secunderabad station to Afzalgunj, a double decker with the number seven, and students of our college had to get off at a stop called Paradise, called so because of its proximity to a garden restaurant of the same name. I went mostly on foot, though, taking the bus perhaps ten or fifteen times through the year. College was a totally new experience. There were about sixty students in my class, an overcrowded classroom. It was a co-educational college. The medium of instruction was English. Our English lecturer was a lady called Mrs Cooper; she was like the Anglo-Indians I had seen in the railway quarters. I liked her accent and paid keen attention to her lectures. Practical classes for physics and chemistry were held in the laboratories. Although I could speak reasonably good English, I had difficulty in approaching teachers since I had no reference to give – the lecturers were more accessible to students whose parents were rich and influential and had good contacts. There was a definite polarization, depending on the students' backgrounds.

My name was at the top of the list of students belonging to the reservation category, and by virtue of the fact that I had decent marks, it was not easy to make out from the list whether I was a student from that category. Two students met me at the gate and whispered, 'Do you belong to the SC?'

Looking them in the eye, I replied, 'Yes.'

From then onwards, they became my friends. These two were Rajesham and Mallesh. Our accent and appearance clearly identified us as Dalits, and we were together till the end of the course. I had some command over English, and was usually able to be a spokesman on their behalf.

Abbasayulu was now transferred to Secunderabad and allotted an officer's quarters at Chilkalguda near Padma Rao Nagar. This house was larger than the one in Rifle Range, with two bedrooms, a large kitchen and a backyard. There were ceiling fans in each room. The bathroom was separate from the lavatory, and there were taps inside the house – the first time we had a water tap inside the house. We shifted here after six years of living in Rifle Range. The household things, though, were the same: we had no furniture, the cots were still rope-woven and the thick home-made cotton-rag rugs were stitched from random pieces of fabric. My mother and sisters-in-law were the designers and makers of these rugs. We had no steel utensils in the kitchen, but whereas my mother had used earthen pots earlier, she now used large aluminium vessels. My father made a small shed in the backyard to serve as the kitchen, and this was the only kitchen in the entire colony from which coal smoke was seen to rise in the early mornings and evenings. We did have an important addition, a radio – an assembled, not branded one, as my father would grumble when he was in a bad mood! – that Mysiah had gifted my brother for the wedding. It was not good to look at, and was a rectangular box with knobs on top, but no matter what it looked like, I used it to the maximum and enjoyed the music, particularly the songs that Radio Ceylon played, and Ameen Sayani's compeering. Balraj too used it regularly.

We lived at Chilkalguda for several years, a large joint family that my father and Balraj oversaw. There were twenty-two members in the family, of whom only three were earning, and most of the rest school-going. Dinner at home was like a small langar, in which masses of people are fed in one go – more than fifteen people would eat at a time as my mother sat in the midst of large bowls serving rice or chapattis, and my sisters-in-law handed filled aluminium plates to each individual.

My mother and I were waiting in a queue in the outpatient ward of King Edward Memorial Hospital, now known as Gandhi Hospital. She was not very well. She was in the habit of taking me along whenever she fell ill and had to consult a doctor. Standing in the queue, my mother said slowly, 'Son, speak in English to the doctor; then he will take good care of me.'

'Okay, Mother. Don't worry,' I told her, looking at her innocent, ailing eyes.

She really believed that the doctors would take greater care if spoken to in English, and was impressed with the way I spoke to the doctor. Like my father, she was proud that I could converse in English. They were especially proud of Abbasayulu, whose command over English was excellent. My father would constantly nag Narsimlu and Anjiah about this, asking them to practise speaking English.

Narsimlu and Anjiah were busy preparing for their supplementary exams to clear the two subjects they had been found lacking in the year before, while I was struggling to cope with the subjects I was not interested in. Father had forced me to take mathematics, physics and chemistry. I was upset, for although I struggled hard, I was not able to get a grip on any of the subjects; mathematics, in particular, appeared to be of a much higher standard. I found physics difficult too. I had no one to seek help from and sometimes felt traumatized. It was constantly on my mind that my father had great expectations of me: next to Abbasayulu, I was the one he had pinned his hopes on. He was very disappointed with Narsimlu and Anjiah, I could see that, but it was amazing that he had not got them to discontinue their studies, and this despite our bad finances. It haunted me day in and day out – I needed to deliver. Then we finally had some good news that relieved the pressure somewhat: my brothers had got through the supplementary exams. Father assured them that he would send them to college for further studies.

Narsimlu was very dynamic, had a wide circle of friends, and was also the leader of the backbenchers in the classroom. Anjiah, on the other hand, had very few friends and preferred to stay at home, which was just as well, because none of our friends dared come to our house when Balraj, the strict disciplinarian, was present. Narsimlu, though, chafed under this discipline, and would often give the slip to Balraj and join his friends. Anjiah, who had grown up to be a mild-mannered and handsome young man, was good at drawing, and had beautiful handwriting. He was an ardent fan of a yesteryear Hindi film hero, Dev Anand, and sported his hairstyle. Abbasayulu liked Anjiah very much. In fact, the three of us were very close, and similar to each other in many respects.

'What happened? Why you are so serious?' asked Balraj of Abbasayulu.

'I have got a transfer as an assistant yard master.'

'Where?'

'In the yard that you work in.' Abbasayulu was disturbed because the assistant yard master is the official under whose direction the shunting master instructs the pointsmen to couple the bogies to make a train.

Balraj was a pointsman, and this meant that Abbasayulu would be the authority to whom Balraj would be answerable.

Father was listening to this conversation, and immediately responded, 'Then apply for leave and try for a transfer to some other place.'

'Father, why?' This was Balraj.

'He cannot work as your boss,' my father said, worried.

Balraj laughed, 'Don't worry, Father, I would be happy to work as my younger brother's subordinate!'

'Oh, no! No, Brother, I can't work as your boss.'

'Take it easy, Brother. We are all working for the railways and you can't be my boss at home. Moreover, it would be thrilling for me to work under you.'

While Abbasayulu was annoyed and embarrassed at the situation, Balraj was proud that his younger brother had reached a stage where he could be his superior. As a pointsman, he had to start half an hour earlier than Abbasayulu each day to take stock of the situation at work. But that was work: at home, he was the supreme authority. Each day, he would quietly slip half an anna under Abbasayulu's pillow, without disturbing his sleep. This was for his tea at work.

Since they worked in the same yard, Balraj and Abbasayulu often had intense discussions at home. Father would intervene at such times, saying they should not bring professional matters home. In fact, my brothers and father were all in the same operating department, and discussing official matters at home was unavoidable at times; occasionally, they also discussed higher officials. I learnt many little details of the work they did from their discussions at home.

I wondered at this strange twist of fate: two brothers working in the same place, and the elder one subordinate to the younger. This, my father explained, was due to the fact that Abbasayulu had got a good education. My father lost no opportunity to point out that it was higher education alone that could help a man to reach greater heights in life. He was sorry for not having been able to educate his eldest son.

As in most Dalit families, witch-hunting, sorcery, and persecution of – and incantations against – evil spirits were common in our family. During the 1960s and '70s in particular, my father, brothers and everyone else in the family had great faith in these customs, and anyone falling sick would more likely be taken to the sorcerer than a doctor. One such incident involved Balraj's daughter Shama, who was about three years old at the time. Shama was running a high temperature and was unable to even open her eyes.

My mother asked, 'Shall we take her to Mantrala Baliah?'

'Yes, that is the best thing to do. The eyelid-hair is straight; she must have been caught by an evil spirit.' This was my father.

Shama was rushed to the Christian cemetery at Mettuguda where Mantrala Baliah lived. This person was not a quack but a sorcerer. At this time, he was almost like a family consultant. He whispered some mantras as he blew on Shama's face, and cut some lemons and circled them around her head. At times he would tie a taweez around the left arm of the sick person too, but not on this instance. The belief was that these practices would scare off the evil spirit that had affected the sick person. But Shama's fever did not abate. Pochamma, my sister-in-law, was very worried: so high was her fever that even the cloth in which the baby was wrapped had become hot. She did not even have the energy to weep. I was awake and by her side the whole of that night, entreating her to take the child to the hospital. In the morning, Abbasayulu took Shama to the hospital. The girl, usually very active, was now motionless. The doctors were appalled at her condition, and very angry with us. They told us that it was a polio attack and that our ignorance had left the baby's left leg almost paralysed, causing a perfectly normal child to become handicapped. My sister-in-law looked at her young daughter and beat her chest; she wailed in the hospital and the doctor had to send her away from the ward. This baby is a young woman today; despite her handicap, and thanks to her determination, she is today a postgraduate degree holder in chemistry, and a lecturer in a government college. She has two young children, and is now a practising Christian.

My second sister-in-law, Krishnaveni, was also a victim of similar superstitions. I now think she had some undiagnosed psychological problem: she would do odd things like getting up in the middle of the night and washing dishes; sometimes, one would find her talking to herself in a strange voice and laughing. My father and older brothers believed that some kind of ghost made her do the weird things. When asked about it in the day, she would say that she was not aware of doing anything at night. Mantrala Baliah had not proved very effective and my father found a new young sorcerer called, strangely, Richard. I wondered how 'Richard' could be a sorcerer and do black magic, since sorcery is not very prevalent among Christians. As fee, he asked for a black goat, some lemons, turmeric powder, black beads and alcohol. Father, Abbasayulu and Krishnaveni prepared to go; I wanted to go along. It was late in the afternoon and my father did not want me to accompany them, but I ended up going since Abbasayulu requested Father on my behalf too.

It was twilight now, and we were waiting at a place full of shrubs and trees, almost like a small jungle (the same place has today been transformed into a park called Indira Park). Richard tied the black goat to the trunk of a small tree. He made my sister-in-law sit before him. Taking a small portion of the hair from the centre of her head, he tied it into a knot, and started burning some camphor and other things in a small earthen bowl in which he had some fireballs, probably hot glowing coal. He began to chant some mantras, and my sister-in-law was now rotating from the waist in a circular motion, making peculiar sounds. The sorcerer now began to beat my sister-in-law with a small bundle of neem leaves and asked her, 'Who are you? Why did you come? Are you a male ghost or female ghost?'

Laughing loudly, and making hiccup-like sounds, she said, 'I am a female ghost, a Brahmin ghost, and I need curd-rice!'

When curd-rice was placed before her, she started eating by the handfuls!

Richard informed us that this was a dangerous ghost and that he would put its soul into the black goat. He gulped the alcohol at a stretch from the bottle and threw the empty bottle away, then sprinkled the turmeric powder on the goat, all the while chanting some mantras. He then threw the goat on the ground and bit its throat with his strong teeth until it died. Even as I was surprised at his strength, my father announced that he had killed the ghost. My sister-in-law had in the meantime fallen unconscious. It was only when we sprinkled water on her face that she regained consciousness. Surprisingly, after this incident, she gradually became normal.

This kind of thing went on in our house for a long time, for my father and Balraj had great faith in such traditions.

Apart from this, we had an annual Durgamma puja to worship Goddess Durga. The whole night, a priestly man would conduct the puja with his assistant, to the rhythm of the ritualistic beating of drums. My mother would sit in front of this man as he invoked the spirit of Durga in her, and she would go into a trance. Our neighbours of the upper castes, Brahmins included, would close their doors and stay in; in these quarters for Class III employees, they did not know that we were untouchables and thought we were Sudras who observed strange rituals. They were terribly afraid of the chanting and beating of drums. In the early morning, after narrating a story to the accompaniment of the drum, the priest would slaughter a goat and sprinkle the blood all around, to drive away evil forces. This, father said, was bali. This would be followed by a feast. Now I wonder about this: I see some similarities to the Vajrayana Buddhist practice where the Dalai Lama draws a geometrical design using different colours on the ground, just as the priest did.

The much awaited results of my PUC were announced. I was not surprised at the results – I had got through the exams in the third division. My father was very unhappy and so were my elder brothers. I had not expected even this, however, and was happy that I had not lost a year. We were to study further, and Abbasayulu helped us plan what we would do. He made the effort to secure admission for us to an undergraduate course. All three of us – Narsimlu, Anjiah and I – were to study for the BSc course, and went by Abbasayulu's advice regarding our choice of subjects. I was to opt for a combination of mathematics, physics and chemistry, while Narsimlu and Anjiah opted for botany, zoology and chemistry. They had lost a year; so all of us were at the same level. I took admission in Nizam College, while they continued at the Secunderabad College of Arts and Science.

Nizam College, once known as Jagirdars' College, was the best-known college in the area in those days. This institution produced some of the finest bureaucrats, industrialists, politicians and diplomats of that era. It is reputed even today, and top-ranking officials, industrialists, business people and politicians prefer to send their children here. I was fortunate to get admission there; Abbasayulu was glad that I had received an offer of a place in such a prestigious institution and argued with Balraj against sending me to Secunderabad College, where too I had secured a place.

It was the beginning of my pursuit of higher learning, and my immediate problem was how to get to college every day. I would have to travel from Secunderabad to Basheer Bagh, a long distance, and it meant going over the Tank Bund. My father advised me to go on a bicycle, which I was against. It was too long a distance, and no friend of mine rode a bicycle. I went on foot for a few days, until Balraj arranged a bus pass for me. The cost of the bus pass was not even ten rupees a month in those days, but for a family like ours, it was a fair sum of money. The bus I took was a Number 7, a double-decker, and this was the bus I travelled in for three years.

I made new friends in the college. I found that, as the saying goes, birds of the same feather flock together. There were clear groups: students coming in cars would make friends with others like themselves, and those riding motorbikes were in a group of their own. Rural feudal lords' sons, mostly Reddys, made a distinct group; they spoke among themselves only in the vernacular and had an inferiority complex as far as English was concerned. Nor was their Hindi good, unlike the local students. My own group was a small one consisting of those from the lower rungs of the economic hierarchy. Janaki Manohar, the first friend I made at Nizam, was sitting in the last row when I entered the classroom the first time. I sat by him and introduced myself as Satyanarayana. He called me 'Satyam' from the beginning, and all my friends now called me by that name. I made other friends too, including K.N. Srinivas Rao, Ravi Prakash, Bharadwaj and Shanmugham. Of all, I was closest to Manohar. Shanmugham took the same bus that I did. His father was a ghee merchant and it was clear that the family had a heavy breakfast in the mornings – for Shanmugam would board the bus and fall asleep immediately! I often had to wake him up when we arrived at our destination.

It was close to the end of the first year. Manohar and I were standing under a big tamarind tree, talking about his plans to visit his native place, Warangal, during the vacation. Another of my friends, Dharma Raj, came running towards me. Dharma Raj was, like me, from a Dalit family. Almost dragging me away from Manohar, he whispered into my ear, 'Arey, Satyam, I saw the list of scholarship holders in the office and it has your name on it. Do you belong to the scheduled caste?'

'Yes, so what?'

'Let us go to the clerk and request him not to display the list on the notice board, lest all our friends come to know, and belittle us.'

He was correct; nobody knew about our caste here. We rushed to the office. Dharma Raj spoke to the clerk and the list was never put up on the board. I received the scholarship – as did my brothers, belonging as we did to the scheduled castes – and from this money, we were able to buy a pair of clothes and shoes for each of us, which we wore for the first time at the end of first year. My father used every single paisa of our scholarship money towards no other purpose but to cater to our needs.

It was in my second year of college that my father took voluntary retirement. He sat alone at the backyard with a worried look on his face one day. Mother quietly went to him and asked in a low voice, 'What happened, Balraja? Why are you so tense?'

He mumbled, 'I went to the doctor for a check-up and they found me unfit.'

Both were silent for a while; my mother was upset. He continued, 'They want to move me to a less important job, one where a vision test is not required. We should consult our sons.'

'How will things be, then? Shall we get our sons to drop out?' my mother asked, troubled.

Father was terribly upset on hearing it said so plainly, although he knew that my mother was right to fear. All his dreams appeared to have been shattered. The issue was discussed by Father, Mother, Balraj and Abbasayulu. Father was prepared to continue working at a less significant job on a lower pay so that we could continue our education. My brothers, however, were of the opinion that he should not take up the job on a reduced pay.

'Father, there is no need for you to work as peon,' said Balraj.

'But, Son, your brothers have to go to college ...'

'We assure you, Father, we will take up that responsibility,' Abbasayulu said.

'It will be difficult to support the family if I sit at home,' my father was stating a fact.

'No, Father, we can't bear to see you working as peon. There won't be a problem. We shall take care of everything,' said Balraj.

Between them, Balraj and Abbasayulu convinced Father not to work any more and so he decided to opt for voluntary retirement. It was a painful decision for him, and he regretted it for the rest of his life.

On our part, we made an effort to minimize the burden on our brothers by using books from the library instead of buying them.

Abbasayulu was a matriculate and an officer in the railways, but he had a lingering desire to study further when he saw us going to college. Although by this time he had three little daughters, he joined the PUC at Secunderabad College and attended classes by opting for night duty. I felt strange and excited when he began to sit with us during the study hours. The house actually turned academic in the evenings, with almost everyone holding a book. Although his subjects were different from mine, Abbasayulu would quite often share the notes he had taken in the classroom with me, confident that I would be able to make suggestions on his use of English. His children often disturbed him, but that did not shake his determination. Father made sure that the radio was not played in the evenings.

It was a Murphy radio we now had, one that Balraj had bought.

Now that we were in college, our friends were allowed to visit us. Most of the visitors were Narsimlu's friends – unlike Anjiah and me, he had a big gang of friends, several of whom came from business families.

We had little money to spend, whereas a few of our friends were in a position to spend money liberally. Balraj would give me a rupee as pocket money for the month – today when I tell my daughters this, they laugh at me, 'Oh, come on, Dad, tell us something we can believe!' Yes, by their standards, it is unbelievable, but for me in those days, it was a significant amount, and I spent it very carefully. Four of us went out for a cup of tea at Olympia Hotel at Gunfoundry each day, and my turn to pay would come every fourth day. The tea cost five paise per cup, and each of us had to pay twenty paise by turns. Sometimes, I thought of not drinking tea, for there were days when I would have no money, but Manohar would pay on my behalf. We would listen to music played on the gramophone records as we drank tea.

I still found mathematics tough. Manohar was good at it, though; we would sit in his house on Sundays and he would help me with it. Physics and chemistry were somewhat better: I could memorize the lessons there, even if I could not follow them at times.

My father had no earnings now. He was dependent on my brothers even for his local cigars, and my brothers took care of his needs meticulously, providing all that he required. Nevertheless, my father was morose. For a while, though, he was kept busy making trips to the railway office for his service settlements.

It was evening and we were returning home one after the other. My father was awaiting my younger brothers when Balraj rushed in with a piece of paper in his hand. He was breathing hard.

'What happened, Son?' Father asked anxiously.

'It's a telegram,' my brother said, trying to be calm.

'About what?'

'Grandfather ... is no more.' There was a shiver in his voice.

The news came as a great shock. My father slumped heavily on the ground, holding his head. Mother started wailing loudly, beating her chest; my brothers and I started crying. Grandfather's life had come to an end – the untouchable from Vangapalli who had not turned back after burying his wife in the village had now bid his final farewell. Had he not joined the railways, the history of our family would have been different. His demise was painful to us. Even now, I am often reminded of how I enjoyed it when he took me with him while he tended our goats. We rushed to Nekonda, my aunt's place, where he had breathed his last. Father, being the eldest son, performed the last rites. He stayed in Nekonda for ten days to complete the rituals.

Father's service accounts were finally settled. He got a few thousand rupees from his provident fund and gratuity. At that time, there were no pension benefits in the railways. However, my father became more self-confident since he had some money now. I frequently saw him and my older brothers going to the toddy or arrack shop together like friends and returning drunk.

'Bidda, I will go to my village, Vangapalli,' my father said one such night.

'But why?' my eldest brother asked.

'You know we have our ancestors' land; your great-grandfather owned several acres. I want to claim it and engage in agriculture.'

'Oh, no, Father, don't waste your money. There is a big building in Walker Town. Why don't you purchase it with the money you have instead?' said Abbasayulu. This was something of a dream, and not really possible; something he wouldn't have suggested if he was sober.

Father looked at him seriously and said, 'No! Should I purchase the house for you to quarrel amongst you after my death? I have given all of you a good education and you are free to purchase houses for yourselves; let me claim the land of our ancestors that my father left.'

Although my father was in a drunken state, he was practical in his thinking. The three debated the issue till my mother intervened.

The next morning, Father seriously considered his plan. He wanted to go to his village and take up agriculture. My mother argued against it – she had her doubts about getting hold of the land. Despite no one being in favour of the idea, my father was firm in his resolution. He strongly held the hope that he would be able to reclaim the land. He sounded out his brother, Yelliah, who encouraged him. The two of them decided to go to Vangapalli.

I completed my second year of BSc and passed in the second division. Narsimlu and Anjiah got through too. We all found the final year very tough. Meanwhile, Abbasayulu joined Secunderabad College for his BA. He was a role model – indeed, he was the best of all of us. He had to face many odds, having taken up studies once again, but none of the obstacles deterred him from the pursuit of learning.

Though my father did learn to read and write a little, we are the real first-generation learners in our family. My father's strong determination that we should pursue higher studies at any cost was what helped us achieve that goal. Untouchable families had been kept away from learning for centuries; and so, having been forced to serve people of other castes for generations together, having never learnt to question or nurture independent thought, their minds were unprepared. Fallow land needs a lot of effort for cultivation – ploughing, watering, seeding and weeding. So also a mind that has been stagnant for centuries needs great effort to become receptive to knowledge. We were not as comfortable with learning as our children are; our circumstances were different. My father's friends were mostly illiterate and our interaction with them was not educative; our environment at home was the same as that of any other Dalit family. Access to knowledge through any media was far beyond our reach. There was nothing like getting together with learned people to imbibe knowledge from them, a facility that we were able to give our children. Under these conditions, we had to struggle hard. Every step we took was under difficult situations, whether in the classroom or outside. We had little confidence and an inferiority complex haunted us at every step.

We wrote the final year examinations in the summer of 1965. I was doubtful of passing in mathematics, and my fears proved to be justified. Narsimlu and Anjiah failed too – in botany. So not even one of the three of us passed the examination. The family was grief-stricken. My sisters-in-law tried to console me, but since I had a foreboding, I was not terribly distressed. Similarly with Narsimlu and Anjiah. The only thing I was worried about was whether I would be allowed to complete the course by attempting the exam once more. There was much discussion in the house on this and Abbasayulu came to our rescue, arguing that we should take the supplementary examinations and get another chance. When I thanked my brother, he only said that he would send me on for postgraduate studies if I passed.

In those days, my mother would sometimes visit her aunt who lived in an outhouse in one of the big bungalows at Domalguda near Liberty Theatre, which has recently been converted into a shopping plaza. This lady was my grandmother's sister and made her living as a household help. She was very attached to my mother and would occasionally drop by too. We would visit her often and when making such calls, my mother would accompany me in the morning on a Number 7 bus. We would get off at Liberty and walk a short distance to reach my grand-aunt's place. My mother would look curiously at the buildings on either side of the road and ask me, 'Bidda, will you build such buildings when you become an officer? I want to see that!'

I would gaze at my mother's hopeful face, which told me that she believed that her sons would fulfil her desire. Smiling back, I would say, 'Definitely, Mother.'

She had big dreams, and she had a right to them. She had played a major role in giving us an education, toiling her life away working as an agricultural labourer in the fields. I wished that her dream would turn into reality, and that we would be able to provide her a comfortable life. She was quite attached to me since she believed that I had saved her life as a child. She had cysts around her breast which, people told her, were likely to threaten her life. Once, her breast was filled with milk and she suffered from unbearable pain; on her insistence, I suckled her breast, which she believed had cured the problem.

'Namaste, Patela, hope you had no problems finding the house,' my father welcomed a man clad in a white dhoti and striped shirt. He seemed to have come from a village.

'Aaa! Ramaswamy; yes, it was quite easy to find your house,' said he, handing his bag to my father.

Except my father, we were all surprised by the unexpected arrival of this stranger. Balraj was almost ready to leave for work. Turning to him, my father said, 'Bidda, this is Narsimha Rao, the patel of our village, Vangapalli. He wanted to meet you all.'

My brother smiled at the man, offering him a seat. I brought him a glass of water. In the next room, my mother questioned my father in low tones, asking him about the stranger.

'Balraja, who is that man?'

'He is our village patel. When I met him in our village, he promised to help us,' my father said.

'How can he stay with us untouchables,' my mother asked, innocently. Patels belonged to a higher caste.

'No one knows him in this place, and he is a nice man,' my father laughed.

The man bathed and changed into fresh clothes. Talking in friendly tones with my father and assuring my mother that he would help Father get back his share of land, he seemed a good person. My father treated him as a special guest and offered him a good drink and a variety of non-vegetarian food. The man was happy with our hospitality.

When Abbasayulu came in from night duty the next morning, he was surprised to see a stranger in the house. He said to me, 'Satti, who is the man sleeping there?'

'He is Patel Narsimha Rao from Vangapalli.'

'What is he doing here?' he asked in a serious tone.

'He's here to help Father get back our land.'

My brother was thoughtful as he went into the other room to change his clothes.

The patel stayed with us for three days, enjoying our hospitality and visiting different places in the twin cities. On the last day, he advised my father to go to the village at the earliest and build a hut adjacent to our land. This, he maintained, would strengthen my father's claim to the land.

'Dora, will they allow me to do so?' my father asked, a little wary.

'Why not? I shall personally stand by while you build a hut, and if you live there for a few months, I shall settle the matter by taking it to the panchayat.'

My father was relieved to hear this and became hopeful of getting back the land. Seeing the patel off, my father promised him that he would go to the village at the earliest.

My father had some money now, and some confidence; and he had a strong desire to acquire his great-grandfather's land. He wanted to settle down in the village with my mother and cultivate the land. Mother was least interested and tried to discourage him.

'Father, will we really get the land?' I asked him when he returned from the station.

'Of course!'

'What will you do with it, Father?' I asked.

He looked at me as though I were a fool.

'It is our ancestral property and we have a right to it. Moreover, I am now free of formal occupation; I can work in the fields and raise a good crop.'

'Is that so? Can you actually cultivate land?' I was surprised to learn this.

My father smiled at me and said, 'Yes, my son. I used to work as an agricultural labourer before I joined the railways; and now when you and your brothers have to study further and require money, I can try to make a living in our village.'

I was surprised at the strength of my father's determination – in spite of our bad performance – to send us for higher studies. I could see that his desire to acquire the land stemmed partly from the goal of earning some money to pay for our studies. I felt ashamed of the way we had performed but, at the same time, knew that we were making a sincere effort. If we failed, it was because we were unable to get a grip on the subjects we were studying. What kept us going was the encouragement we got from our family.

The day the three of us became the first set of graduates in the Yelukati family, my father was exultant: he celebrated by drinking to his heart's content.

'Balraja, our sons have passed the exams, I shall make them study further!' he told my mother.

She, observing his drunken condition, was very angry. 'If you drink so heavily, you won't be able to, will you? They've studied enough; let them work now.'

My father did not discuss the matter further at this time; he went to bed after being persuaded to eat a little.

October 1967. My father had built a big hut in Vangapalli, by the side of a huge open well, as advised by the patel, and after the Dussehra celebrations my parents and younger sister moved to Vangapalli. My father also furnished the house well. People from the neighbouring

huts peeped in from time to time and were impressed at the sight of the
neatly arranged things in the hut. In the evenings, almost each day, some
people from the village would gather near the hut, and thus interaction
grew. To strengthen relations, my father would offer them toddy. We
had a sewing machine that my sister used, and it was placed such that
one could easily see it on entering the house. It turned out to be a great
attraction, along with two chairs and two cots, which were comparatively
rare possessions in the village. My younger sister, Lakshmibai, with her
city look, was much liked by the ladies and they would watch her every
move. Sometimes, while she worked on the sewing machine, they would
question her about life in the city.

My father wanted us fresh graduates to stay there for a short spell,
and we assented. When we arrived, I roamed around the hut while my
brothers went out. Just outside, I could see the well. It was circular, with
a diameter of more than ten feet. Its inner walls were made of stone. It
had a large pulley fixed to a wooden frame on the edge of the well, over
which a rope could be drawn. Each morning, I watched curiously as
water was drawn from the well to irrigate the paddy fields. Two bullocks
were yoked together, and a thick, strong rope was tied to the yoke. At
the other end of the rope was a huge bucket, and its narrow bottom was
connected to a long leather tube almost as wide as an elephant's trunk.
The rope itself was drawn through the pulley. The bullocks would be
made to walk back and forth over a slope. As they walked away from the
well, the bucket would fill with water and be pulled up, while the leather
tube would fold up. The tube would be pulled by means of another
rope attached to it, and this made the bucket tilt and empty the water
into the tube, from where it flowed into a channel that led to the paddy
fields. The bullocks would walk backwards, causing the bucket to dip
back into the water. A man could, by stopping or releasing the water
flow at different points using his spade, manage to water tens of acres
of paddy fields in a matter of three to four hours! It was a traditional
and ingenious method of irrigating the fields.

My father would meet Patel Narasimha Rao every day. But here, they stood at a distance while speaking. There were many negotiations. The land was in the possession of my grandfather's nephews, and they were not prepared to give it up; in fact, they refused to budge an inch from their stand. When my father wanted to take legal recourse, the patel asked my father to wait for some more time, saying that it was not a wise step to take. My grandfather had been absent from the land for more than fifty years, and the case would be weak. However, Father was insistent, and his brother supported him. They filed a case at the district court in Huzurabad.

We had spent four months in the village when Abbasayulu sent word for us to come back. He wanted us to apply for postgraduate studies; my father sent us back to Secunderabad without wasting a day. He advised us to go ahead and study further, and asked us not to worry about failure. On the train, I was preoccupied by the thought of my father's decision to live in his father's village in order to earn enough to pay for our higher education. I also knew that he was not comfortable living on the earnings of my brothers, but my worry was whether I would be able to rise to his expectations. As it was, we had caused enough heartbreak and expense by failing once. I was shaken out of my reverie by Narsimlu.

'Satti, get up, there is a TC (ticket collector) on the other side. We are reaching Kazipet; let's get off the train before he comes here.' I got up quickly and went to the door to get down on the platform. Like the children of most other railway employees, we used to travel without tickets. If a TC asked us for tickets, we would simply say 'Staff children'. Most TCs were liberal, and at most would make us get off before reaching our destination, and we would have to take another train. Sometimes, the parents would inform the TCs well before the train was due to start, and in such cases we did not have to worry at all.

When we reached home, we learnt that Abbasayulu had passed his BA. We were overjoyed. The academic year 1967–68 was a very significant year for the family; four of Baliah's sons took admission in postgraduate courses, one in the social science stream and three in the pure sciences. Even Abbasayulu had poor knowledge as to what courses were required in job markets and what courses we ought to take. I decided to take chemistry in my MSc course, as I had obtained good marks in my bachelor's; Narsimlu opted for botany and Anjiah for zoology. Abbasayulu took admission to MA in sociology. He continued to work in the railways as an assistant stationmaster.

It was a new chapter for us. Baliah had made it his life's mission to enable his children to undertake higher education. In most Dalit families even from the railways, it was difficult for the children to even reach matriculation. From Secunderabad to Kazipet, people were talking about my father: he had earned a name for sending his children to postgraduate colleges. Even the higher officials in the railways had great respect for my father though he had been at the lowest level of railway employees.

In the same year, Yadagiri joined the engineering course in the Osmania University campus. Yadagiri was my most intelligent sibling. A fair-complexioned, handsome boy, Yadagiri was different from us all. Unlike the rest of us, he was good at mathematics and always stood first in class. By the time he entered middle school, a serious and regular study atmosphere had been established in the house. We had a radio and subscribed to a newspaper, and these gave him access to the world in general – something that we, the older ones, had not had as children. He passed his higher secondary exams with flying colours, and got admission into the engineering college at Osmania University, the only engineering college functioning in Telangana in the 1970s, apart from the Regional Engineering College at Warangal. And he got in on his own merit, without the need to avail of reservation. We celebrated his entry into a professional college since he was the first in our family to go for such a course. He being a very intelligent, lovable boy, Balraj often ended up giving him extra money! He was attached to our mother and one would always find him sitting by her side. He would call her 'Mummy', which made her very happy.

But he would also always argue on trivial matters. As a child, he dreamt of a life of luxury. He hated being poor, and was not happy with the way we lived. He constantly spoke of his rich friends and commented how good their life was. At home, he would even skip a meal if the food was not to his satisfaction, and although it must have been difficult, Mother tried hard to please him. But as he grew older, his thinking changed, and like many engineering students in those days, Yadagiri was attracted to leftist ideology.

One day I was surprised to see my father at the door of the college laboratory. He was on a visit from the village and was wearing a white dhoti with a white shirt and a blue blazer – clothes he wore on important occasions. He smiled at me as my professor granted me permission to meet him. He looked me over and seemed proud by what he saw. He said, 'Son, I came to see you and the new college.' But seeing my anxiety, he asked me to go back to my class.

At dinner, I found that Father had left Mother and my younger sister in the village. This made me sad. Later, he told us how the patel had helped, by standing by as the hut was being built, ensuring that no one dared talk against us.

'Father, are we going to get the land?' asked Balraj.

'Yes, Son, I've even filed a case at the district court in Huzurabad.'

'Father, your father left your village a long time ago, leaving the land. Your own people are eking out a livelihood on it now. Don't you think it unjust to seize the land so?' This was my brother, Yadagiri.

Father was very angry, 'Shut up! What do you know? It is our ancestral property; we have every right to it. Do not interfere when the elders are talking!'

Yadagiri avoided my father's eyes and slipped out of the room. I inwardly agreed with Yadagiri, but Father was bent upon claiming the land. His brother Yelliah also supported him, and so did my two eldest brothers. He left for the village the next day.

In the Class III-type railway quarters where we lived, our family was the largest, with fifteen children between three sets of parents, and in all, it was a family of twenty-one. The quarters, meant for a single family, was occupied by three big families. I now wonder how we managed! Balraj had seven children; Abbasayulu three. In the evenings, the room where we studied would be overcrowded with all of us studying – some reading aloud and some writing – and no one minding another. My sister-in-law would only serve dinner after we completed our assignments.

Balraj's word was the unwritten law. He was a strict disciplinarian and one had to invariably take his permission before going out.

The period spanning 1968–69 was one of crisis. At this time, there was an upsurge, a mass movement for a separate Telangana, which took a political turn. It caused us to lose an academic year, but opened a new chapter in my life. Colleges were closed, and it was at this time that I received a letter from the Zilla Parishad offering me work as a teacher in a village school. The Zilla Parishad was an autonomous administrative body at the district level. There was a system in place whereby every graduate was registered with the state's employment exchange, and this provided such administrative bodies a pool from which to draw candidates for whatever jobs were available.

'Chinnanna, I have received an offer from the Zilla Parishad to work as a teacher,' I told Abbasayulu, showing him my appointment order.

'Satti, go and work; it is an opportunity for you,' my brother said. I must have looked doubtful, for he continued, 'Look, Satti, you have no college now; all the colleges are closed. You will gain some work experience working in the village.'

I agreed with that reasoning and decided to go to Karnakota, the village where the school needed a teacher. My mother, who was in Secunderabad at this time, heard us talking and vehemently opposed the idea upon learning the name of the village. Karnakota was then well known for witch-hunting, sorcery, black magic, etc., and Mother was terribly afraid for me. It took great effort to convince her. She ultimately consented on condition that I must leave without the slightest delay if I faced any problems. When I left, however, she wept to see me go.

I carried only a small suitcase. It was a new experience for me to leave my large family, and particularly Narsimlu and Anjiah. I had to take a train to Tandur and from there, a bus to another village, from where I had to go on foot to reach Karnakota – the village had no bus service. It was located far from the large and more accessible areas, and did not even have electricity. Balraj and Abbasayulu came to see me off. Balraj was not happy with the situation and tried to discourage me right until the last minute. I had made up my mind, however. But even I was in tears when the train started moving away from the platform. I saw that my brothers were also wiping their eyes, and I heard them say, 'Drop us a letter when you get there.'

The train reached Tandur in the afternoon. I got into a crowded bus and reached a village close to Karnakota soon after. A few passengers were going to the same village and I followed them. Across fields we went, they and I, with a suitcase in my hand. It was a tough task, for the black soil there was very sticky and slippery. It seemed to have rained the previous night. My shoes kept getting stuck in the mud, and it was difficult to even lift them clear off the mud; I finally removed them and walked barefoot, sometimes balancing the suitcase on my head. It was an unforgettable experience, and I thought of it as a test I had to undergo before I started living on my own. Finally, we arrived.

The Zilla Parishad High School was a new L-shaped building, a little way from the main part of the village. It was closing time, and the boys and girls were chattering as they left the school. The headmaster, Narsimha, surveyed me and my soiled trousers as I handed him my appointment order.

'Oh! You are from the city; a graduate! I think you might have by this time seen how far in the interiors the place is.' His tone suggested he was not confident of my staying there.

'Yes, sir,' I said.

'You are from Hyderabad. Have you decided to live here?' He expressed his doubt without hedging.

'I shall stay, sir.' I was expressing far greater confidence than I felt!

'Okay ... you will have to sleep in the school tonight and tomorrow, and the students or the staff will look for accommodation for you.'

The watchman took my suitcase and led me into the library, whose long tables I was to use as my cot for the night.

The next morning, I went round the village and was surprised to see that it was located in and around a big fort, whose only gate had strong wooden doors about twenty feet high. Within the fort were more than three hundred houses; about as many dotted its periphery. Round the village ran a large, deep pit, perhaps originally a moat dug to protect it from enemies. The houses in the village – and as I later found out, of most villages around – were built of stone, the kind popularly known as Shahabad stone. The area was full of stone quarries, and while this stone was extensively used for flooring in city houses, here, even the walls and roofs were built of it. A few yards from the gate of the fort, under a huge peepul tree, was a temple dedicated to Lord Hanuman, which the villagers said was more than a hundred years old. I was told that early in the morning, a big cobra would climb to the top of the tree and spread its hood, worshipping the sun-god. I was amazed to hear this; there would be more stories in later days, some of them spine-chilling!

Hanumanthu, a fifth-class student, found me a room to live in – a spacious one. I taught the children of the village, and though I was there only for a short spell, the village was a teacher to me. I learnt many lessons there that helped me later in life, including how to live on my own.

One thing I lied about was my caste. My brother had suggested that I keep my caste a secret, lest I find no place in the new village. Untouchability was still prevalent and strictly followed in villages. I was to say that I was a Tenugu, a Sudra. I took the risk of hiding my caste, which meant that I lived in danger of being found out every day. Villagers belonging to the Tenugu community often visited me and enquired about my family and marital status, some even inviting me to dinner. I would constantly worry that someone would find out that I was an untouchable. Had the villagers known my real caste, at best, they would have driven me out of the village with contempt. I shudder to think of the worst-case scenario.

The school was new and had good infrastructure. The library books and laboratory equipment were still packed when I joined. I was the only graduate teacher in the school; the rest, including the headmaster, were secondary grade matriculate trained teachers. In general, the villagers had great respect for teachers, whom they would address respectfully as 'Master'. I was respected not only because I was a graduate, but also because I was from the city. I was assigned to teach the higher classes; general science and mathematics were the subjects I taught.

I kept myself busy with school activities. Once, I was explaining the properties of oxygen to the students of tenth class when a girl asked, 'Sir, how can you explain the properties of something that you don't see?'

I was surprised by her question, which had a valid point. 'You can feel it,' I said.

'You can feel the air, yes, but that consists of many gases.' She was not satisfied with my answer.

'It can be identified by testing its properties,' I said and promised to demonstrate it the following day. The students were happy to hear that.

That evening, I checked to see if all the equipment and chemicals necessary for the preparation of oxygen were available. The next morning, I demonstrated the preparation of oxygen by means of an experiment, and conducted the relevant tests on the oxygen produced. It was the first time a practical demonstration had been conducted in the school. Although what I had done was nothing great, the students were enormously impressed, and even the teachers congratulated me. Soon, everyone in the village was talking of me. I became a very popular teacher, and well known even in schools outside the village! Students would pour into my room in the evenings and the village heads began to invite me for dinner. In a very short period, I had created a space for myself in the school and the village.

Sometimes in the evenings the teachers and students would play volleyball. The boys became attached to me. I was never left alone in my room, even at night – knowing my terrible fear of snakes, some students would sleep in my room. Snakes were common there, and often found their way into houses as well. The local people were not afraid of them, and the snake charmers would easily catch them. They had remedies for snake bites too. Hanumanthu, the student who had found me my room, took it upon himself to look after my requirements, almost like a personal assistant! Despite warnings, he would skip classes to cook food for me. Needless to say, I developed a liking for the boy.

It was a Sunday. I was reading a book when Hanumanthu said, 'Master, let us go swimming; there is a big open well close by.' Several other students had gathered around too.

'No, I do not know how to swim,' I said.

'Don't worry, sir, we will teach you,' all of them said in chorus. I was hesitant, and afraid, but they insisted.

'Let us go, sir; it is hot. While we swim, we will teach you to swim too.' Hanumanthu was already taking out a dhoti for me, and I followed them despite not being in favour of the idea.

We reached a big open well, with steps that descended into the water. The students began to dive in – all of them were perfect swimmers. Some began to play a game in the water, trying to catch one another while they swam; others went deep, and rose to the surface only after several seconds, which made me a little anxious. Hanumanthu tied a dhoti around my waist, as if it were a long rope, and asked me to get into the water using the steps. I was sitting on the edge, beating my legs in the water, when someone suddenly pushed me into the water. I was horrified, and felt I was drowning, but they had pulled me out by the dhoti tied around my waist in a second. I sat on the steps, scolding and cursing the boys. Hanumanthu and the other boys laughed, telling me that it was the only way to get rid of the fear of drowning and start learning to swim. I took their point and started to make a real attempt to learn, swimming close to the edges while they held me by the dhoti. In a few weeks, I had learnt how to swim, and soon made it a practice to go swimming every Sunday.

The people who came to my room would quite often talk of ghosts, and how they moved in the night: you can hear the sounds of tiny bells from their anklets, they said.

'Master, yesterday I went to answer the call of nature on this side of the village, beyond the school, but to my surprise, found myself on the opposite side, a mile away!' Mogulappa said. Mogulappa was an adult, and visited me frequently. I even tutored him upon request.

'How did that happen?' I was quite surprised.

'It was a ghost that carried me, master,' he said as he chewed on his betel nut. Such stories annoyed me, but made me a little apprehensive too.

Ramulu, the owner of the house I lived in, was a sorcerer. Sometimes in the evenings, he would sit with me for hours together, telling me about the people who practised sorcery and black magic, and how they got rid of ghosts that entered people's bodies.

'Master, you are very intelligent; I will teach you mantras. They will help you serve the poor when you return to your city,' said Ramulu one day.

This amused me and I smiled at him, which he took as a sign of acceptance.

Though I knew these were superstitions, I was afraid, and a desire to learn sorcery was sprouting in my mind. As the new moon's night approached, Ramulu began to tell me what I had to do. He said it would be a very difficult procedure: one had to dig open a grave and take out the skull. Holding the skull in both hands, one had to sit in the open grave and repeat the mantras. Any mispronunciation of the words could cost one one's life. The very thought of sitting in an open grave holding a skull and chanting mantras without any mistakes sent a chill down my spine, but I didn't back out. On the eve of the day, all arrangements were made, and a man was employed to dig a grave. Ramulu examined me to ensure that I was a suitable student, and then, seeing a mole on my left arm he immediately said, 'Master, it is not possible for me to teach you; you are one of those rare people that are not affected by sorcery or black magic. Nobody can do you any harm by sorcery, neither can you harm anyone by it. This mark on your arm will not allow any sorcery to affect you.'

I was relieved to be freed from the trauma of it all; just a little while before, I had in my mind been cursing the day this crazy idea had entered my head!

Ramulu asked, 'Master, did you sleep in the school building all alone that first night?'

'Yes, what of it?'

'Now I understand. The school has deadly ghosts. Had it been someone else, he would have died!' He laughed.

I was annoyed, and hoped what Ramulu asserted was wrong.

I would visit my family regularly, generally in the first week of the month. On one such visit, I had reached very late the previous night, and got up quite late the next morning. As I had my tea, I saw Father approaching me, a severe look on his face. I was suddenly afraid and could not look into his eyes.

'Satti, where was the need for you to go to the village to work?' My father was fuming; his eyes were red.

I realized that he was afraid that I might discontinue my studies. 'Father, I did not want to sit idle. The college is closed now, and when it reopens, I shall immediately leave the job and take up my studies again.'

At that, he cooled down and said, 'Son, when you start earning, you begin to lose interest in studies. That's what I am afraid of.'

'I assure you, Father, I shall complete my course,' I promised him.

It was now several months since Father had moved to the village. He had spent a large amount on the litigation, and the case was going against him. He had no tax receipts of the land. After several hearings, the judge gave his verdict, which went against my father; he also had to bear the costs of the entire litigation. The same night, my father took away most of the things from the hut and they left the place. They were very upset: my father had lost all his money, and my mother had lost her health. We found out that she had developed diabetes. The defeat was a great shock for my father, and it took a long time for him to recover from it.

I felt sorry for Father and wished to be by his side. I wanted to give up my job, and decided to do so as soon as the academic year ended.

It was almost the end of the school year, and the annual examinations were almost over when I received a telegram from home: 'YADAGIRI MISSING STOP START IMMEDIATELY'

It was a great shock: the very thought of my brother leaving the house made me weep. I rushed to the headmaster with the telegram and with his consent, wasted no time, packed my luggage, and bid goodbye to Hanumanthu, who had taken such good care of me. And thus I left the village and the people who taught me to live on my own.

On the bus, I wondered why Yadagiri might have left and where he might have gone, till I could think no more.

Yadagiri's disappearance was a big jolt. He was in his second year of engineering studies when he disappeared. He had left home as usual, carrying Balraj's dinner for him, and that was the last any of my family had seen him. A police complaint had been lodged, but to no avail.

My mother was distraught and broke down on seeing me, 'Your brother has gone, and it is more than a week since he's been seen.' Holding me tight, she rested her head on my shoulder and wept. Seeing her in such a state, I could not control myself; my eyes were wet as I tried to console my mother. We were sunk in grief. The radio did not play for a number of days, and at every little noise, my mother would look expectantly at the door.

My father was not at home when I arrived. He had gone to Bombay in search of Yadagiri. He was frantic, and later, when he did not find Yadagiri there, he searched for him in other big cities like Madras and Calcutta as well, going around holding his photograph. On his return, he approached holy men, soothsayers and priests, constantly praying for the return of my brother. Every effort proved futile; Yadagiri's disappearance remained a mystery, and was very painful for all of us. No one spoke harshly of him and we all wondered what made him leave the house. It was the most tragic incident in our family. Apart from the personal loss, we had also lost a highly intelligent and promising young man who might have become the first engineer in the family.

In 1970, my sister Lakshmibai got married. It was still a huge family, with only two earning members. Differences began to crop up between the two over petty things, mostly on children's issues, and the difference in wages. The relationship was sometimes strained to the point where my father had to patch things up.

Abbasayulu and I used to have frank discussions on family matters, and I knew that he had decided to live separately since I, Narsimlu and Anjiah had almost completed our courses and were about to begin earning shortly.

'Look Satti, I tried to help the three of you in your education and I am no longer in a position to bear the burden at the cost of my children,' he told me one day, just after I had appeared for my final year postgraduation exams.

'Yes, I know, Chinnanna. You can leave us the moment the three of us get jobs,' I responded.

'Yes, I can wait for a month or two.'

The conversation stopped when we saw my father approaching.

My master's subject was chemistry, and there was a great demand for those trained in the subject in the employment market that year, the reason being that the government had opened a number of junior colleges and there was a dearth of lecturers. I received an appointment for a position at the Government Junior College at Nirmal even before the results were announced. Nirmal was a small town in the Adilabad district surrounded by villages. I was greatly excited since I had been fortunate not to experience unemployment – a situation experienced by many young people after their education, and one that often led to frustration. I did not delay even a day in joining my job and left for Nirmal immediately. With my experience of teaching in a school, I did well at the junior college, although I was still technically underqualified and expecting my PG degree. However, with my city background, I had an edge over the local teachers, and was able to impress students with the way I dressed and spoke. Narsimlu and Anjiah were still unemployed.

Soon, the results were announced; all four of us had cleared the examinations. Father was elated – four of his sons were now postgraduates – and he expressed his joy through a spurt in his social visits, which were basically occasions for him to share the news that his sons had achieved postgraduate degrees. Very soon, Anjiah secured a job as junior lecturer in zoology at a college in Bhainsa, and Narsimlu, who changed his name to Narsing Rao through a government gazette notification, got a job at Dharmavant Junior College, a government-aided college in Hyderabad. There was a big celebration in the family. Three earning members had been added to the family in a matter of months. But it also meant that Abbasayulu and his family would now live separately, and my parents were saddened by this.

Abbasayulu had played a great role in supporting the joint family. We could not have completed our education without his help. He had encouraged us at every step, despite our failures, and left us only when we had started to earn our own living. To add to that, he left us in the quarters that were allotted to him, and moved into a rented house. This brother of mine was my best friend, the first doctorate in the family, and also the first professor.

When Abbasayulu resigned from the railways after putting in twelve years of service, it came as a shock to us, especially to my father who expected him to become a big officer in the railways. His hopes had been raised even further because of the improvement in Abbasayulu's educational qualifications. I had continued to meet my brother regularly, and was rather upset with his resignation too. I wanted to know what had made him resign from a post in which he was so well settled. It worried me also because he now had five children to support and bring up.

'Chinnanna, why did you resign from the railways?'

'Satti, I had decided to leave the railways after completing my MA. I have now joined as a lecturer at Satyamma Narsimha Rao College.'

'But that is a private college and you have no job security!'

'I know I'm taking a risk.'

'It is not worth it; you have children!' I objected.

My sister-in-law, who was offering me tea, was in tears. 'Satyam, look how big a risk he's taking, leaving us insecure.'

'Satti, I took this decision not in haste, but after a lot of thought.

In the railways, which is a vast organization, I may end up as station superintendent, but that is not what I want. I want to become a professor.' He was very firm in his resolve, and I could not move him.

I was happy that he was so confident and no longer really worried, but was still concerned about his present lack of security.

'Do not worry, Vadina,' I comforted my sister-in-law, 'let's hope everything goes well, and that this decision brings him better positions and a better life for all of you.'

One consequence of Abbasayulu's decision was that we had to vacate the quarters allotted to him. We moved back into Balraj's quarters at Rifle Range, and once again had to live in small quarters. With Balraj's seven children, my parents and Narsing Rao, it was a difficult task. Narsing pressed for a bigger house, since we could actually afford to move into one. We did move, but that meant we had to move from the railway colonies that we were used to, to other areas where people of all kinds lived. Finding a house was a bit of a difficulty. People inquired into the caste of a person seeking to rent a house, and it became a problem for us. We ultimately took a house on rent from a Sardarji, and moved to Sitaphalmandi.

My youngest brother and Father's most pampered son, Laxman, did not show interest in studies. In spite of having more resources than we had ever had at our disposal, he was unsuccessful in school due to his negligence of and indifference towards studies. He spent most of his time wandering around with his friends. Although he joined classes for the intermediate exam, he could not clear it, and chose to discontinue his education at this point. He thus had to start his career without a firm educational background. Later, we brothers tried to help him establish a fair price shop, but he failed to run it properly and it ended in a loss.

After making a serious effort, he later found employment in a central government public sector undertaking.

⁕

Balraj's children were all going to school except the infant twins. This was the second generation of school-going children in our family, and they were not at as much a disadvantage as we had been, for they were based in the city which was relatively free from social evils like untouchability. Balraj, though sometimes harsh, was good at heart, and he loved me for I was the only person who made a real attempt at cracking jokes and keeping everyone in good humour.

Now our family was doing well and there were four earning members apart from Abbasayulu, though two of them lived away from home. There was a change in the lifestyle of the family now: there was a change in the food, not only did we now eat chapattis made of wheat flour (although my father would ask for jonne rottelu, rotis made of jowar or sorghum flour, now and then), we had vegetables and rice at every meal. We had more physical comforts too, like writing tables, chairs and ceiling fans.

My father spent much of his time with Anjiah at Bhainsa. Of the six of us, Father was most attached to him, and he too relied much on my father. Father was now looking out for good matches for us, and people of our caste were seeking to meet my father to try and settle alliances. My father, however, took his time, and discussed each proposal with my mother.

⁕

I had been in Nirmal for about five months when I was offered a position at Dharmavant Junior College, where Narsing Rao was already working. I thought it over – being in a government job at Nirmal meant I had a certain security of job and income, and there were other attendant advantages as well, such as a provident fund, medical benefits and a pension to be had at the end of service. However, transfers from one place to another were possible, and I wanted to stay in the city. I joined Dharmavant College in January 1970 as a junior lecturer – against the wishes of my father, for he opposed my move from government service to quasi-government service.

Father wanted us to join government services. In a few months, Narsing was selected for a job in Suryapet Government Junior College. At the same time, I landed a job in the Government Degree College at Godavari Khani. The latter position, of a lecturer at a degree college, was a higher post than that of lecturer in a junior college. This led to a discussion between us as to who would join work in a distant place and who would remain with our parents.

'Satti, one of us has to be here with our parents. Anji is already in Bhainsa and you know that next year this college will also become a degree college.'

'Then you stay here and I will join Godavari Khani as degree lecturer.'

'No, Satti, I have little chance of growth here; they may not take me as a lecturer for the degree section because there is already a senior lecturer in botany. Your chances of growth here are brighter.'

What my brother said was right and he was right in insisting that one of us should stay with our parents. I decided to stay. Meanwhile, my brothers joined the government services.

My father was very unhappy with my decision.

Narsing had the great quality of perseverance, and would not compromise once he was determined to do something, no matter how many attempts he had to make to achieve the goal. When he joined as a lecturer at the junior college, he decided to also undertake research in his subject. His hard work gained him a PhD, and led him to become a professor at Osmania University later in life!

※

The children had left for school, and I could hear Balraj trying to clear his throat in the washroom as I prepared for my class. Father was sitting by my side, and my mother and sister-in-law were busy in the kitchen when a young lady appeared at the door. She seemed about twenty, was fair in complexion, and had obviously been crying. She carried a small cotton bag stuffed with clothes – had she run away from home?

'Who are you?' my father asked.

Balraj came into the room just then, and asked of my father if he knew who she was. The girl trembled at his tone and was unable to say anything. My father brought her a glass of water and gently helped her sit.

She spoke with difficulty, 'I am Varalakshmi. I was sent out of my house ...'

'But why? And why did you come here?' My father was calm; he appeared to understand what it was about.

My brother was impatient, though, and almost shouted, 'What did you come *here* for?'

'Your brother, Narsing Rao ...' she began to sob.

My father asked, 'Has he promised to marry you?'

She gained some confidence and told my father, 'Yes, we love each other and he has promised to marry me.'

'Who are you? What is your caste?' This was Balraj.

'We are Brahmins ...'

Balraj was surprised now and very angry. He took my father into the next room. 'Father, send her away immediately. She's run away from her house and we cannot let anyone from our family marry such a girl. Moreover, she is a Brahmin.'

'Calm down, my son. She is a girl asking for shelter. Her parents have driven her out; she is helpless.'

'So what? We shouldn't give shelter to an unmarried girl! What will our community think of us? I have unmarried brothers!'

'Son, I understand that, but where will she go? If we close our doors, she will go straight to your brother and they will get married. Then what credibility will you and I have in the community?'

My father was tackling the issue with great tact. He did not care which caste the girl belonged to, nor was he apprehensive about what the community would think. He was thinking as a human being. He had not read any of the social reformers, but his compassion led him to appropriate action. He proved that it was not vital to read books but essential to have a humane heart. Though he had not heard of Dr Ambedkar, the saviour and champion of untouchables and a towering personality of the last century, he broke traditions and entrenched customs, and was the first man in our family to open its doors to inter-caste marriages. My father was a visionary and a great man, greater than many intellectuals who claim to be Ambedkarites, and yet remain against inter-caste marriages.

Balraj was not happy when Father asked her in. My mother and sister-in-law took her into the other room and spoke to her. Mother came to Father and asked, 'Balraja, this girl is a Brahmin; should we marry her to our son? Think of our community, and of our other children. What will our community think of us if she is married to our son?'

'Don't worry about the community,' said he. 'Your son is prepared to marry her and has asked her to come to us. Let her stay here until he comes.'

Mother was not happy any more than Balraj, but she chose not to oppose Father.

Varalakshmi, the new entrant in our house, involved herself in the daily chores, trying to please everyone. When I would be about to leave, she would remind me to take my pen and handkerchief, something I found embarrassing. She helped my sister-in-law with the cooking, but the food she cooked was sweet and would have a lot of oil. Although it tasted good, we could not get used to it, and my father instructed my sister-in-law to teach her to cook our way.

Varalakshmi, we learnt, had been known to my brother for the last three years. She was a teacher in a private primary school and was from a lower-middle-class Brahmin family. Her father was a clerk in the railways. My elder sister, Bachamma, had known about their relationship since Narsing Rao, who was close to her and saw her as a source of strength, had confided in her.

Thus, in 1972, we had an inter-caste marriage in our family – another first. A Madiga marrying a Brahmin girl. Weddings require that the parents of both the bride and the bridegroom be present. The bride has to be given away by her father or her brother, but in this case, since the bride's parents were estranged from her, Mrs Bharati, a social activist from Hamal Basti (literally, Porters' Colony) stood in for her mother, and Narsing Rao's friend Ramesh took the place of her brother. The marriage was solemnized at Yadagirigutta, with Narsing Rao and Varalakshmi being joined in matrimony in the abode of Lord Narasimha Swamy to the chanting of mantras. The wedding was not conducted at the foothills, like thirty years ago, when Dalits were kept away from the temples, but close to the sanctum sanctorum.

After the ceremony, I was surprised to find my mother weeping: she was feeling sorry for the bride since her parents were not present.

Now, there was a total change in our lifestyle; education had changed us in many ways. We looked similar to people from the upper castes because of our attire and the way we spoke. In the cities, the identification markers imposed on Dalits elsewhere had almost vanished, with the ladies wearing their saris like caste Hindu women instead of tying them further up so that they only reached the knees. Most of their silver jewellery was replaced by gold. The men, too, were no more half-naked as before, and it became difficult for caste Hindus to recognize Dalits from their appearance.

In the cities, things were fine as long as house owners or landlords, belonging mostly to the higher castes, were unaware of your Dalit identity, but once it was known, you would be harassed until you vacated the house. Concealing our caste was difficult, for although our ways had changed, our relatives, who were frequent visitors, had distinctly Dalit features. This disclosure therefore happened quite often, and then we would be asked to move. It was frustrating to have to move from house to house just because we were Dalits.

My father was much sought after by the parents of marriageable girls since, in our community, ours was then one of the very few educated Dalit families. Anjiah was twenty-eight and I twenty-seven, and our father was eager to get us married soon. Unlike today, youngsters then had little choice in selecting a life partner, unless it was clandestinely done. My father was searching for good matches for us, going out each time his relatives advised him about suitable girls. One family that he visited was that of Siva Ram, whose children were highly educated. Siva Ram was an engine driver, and had three daughters and three sons. Two of his sons were doctors and the third an architect but, like in most Dalit families, his daughters had received education only up to the school level. My father fixed Anjiah's marriage with Siva Ram's daughter Rukmani.

At about this time, I attracted the attention of a high-ranking official in the state government, T.V. Narayana, and his wife T.N. Sadalakshmi, who was a Dalit politician. I was teaching in an undergraduate college and the college principal, Dadey Prasad, was T.V. Narayana's friend. Mr Narayana was much impressed with the way we were educated and employed as teachers in higher education despite my father being a lower-rung employee in the railways. My qualifications and choice of profession also appealed to him, as he too had started his career as a teacher in a school. My father received a proposal for a marriage alliance from them for their daughter Gayatri. Balraj was of the view that we were socially too far down to have an alliance with them; he also thought that the girl might not be comfortable with our living conditions. Father felt that the alliance would help me since Mr Narayana was a high-ranking official. There was much discussion on this issue. There was talk among our relatives that my wedding was to be fixed in a family of people of high stature, and some of them discouraged my father saying that it might not be good for a boy's family to seek a relationship with a girl from a high-profile family. A day was fixed, nevertheless, for my parents to go with some relatives to see the girl.

My family went to their house. The grand arrangements and the large gathering surprised them. They wondered whether they had arrived at the wrong house. Actually, the girl's parents were in a hurry to settle the match, and had made arrangements for an engagement – they were sure that my parents would like the girl and agree to the match immediately. My mother, though of a view similar to Balraj's, liked the girl, and the matter was settled amicably, ending in an engagement. My wedding was fixed for 23 May 1973.

Anjiah's wedding was held just three days before mine, on 20 May, in the Railway Auditorium, and it was very different from the other weddings in our family. It was the grandest of the marriages by far: for the first time, I saw the pandal under which the bride and groom sat decorated with flowers, and a Brahmin priest performing the rituals. Narsing Rao's nuptials were also performed by a Brahmin priest, but that had been because it was at a temple. The gathering now consisted mostly of urbanized people, and the rituals were the same as those followed by caste Hindus.

My wedding was a grand affair too, arranged by my in-laws at the Lady Hydari Club at Basheer Bagh. This place has only recently been torn down. Although they were not very rich, my in-laws were influential people, and a galaxy of important personalities were present at the ceremony. All the staff of my college were present; so were my friends Rama Rao and Subba Rao. We followed Arya Samaj rituals; there were no Brahmins, nor Brahminical rites. My people sat at the back, observing the show. The food was arranged in three halls: one for people who preferred to sit and eat, the other a buffet-style dinner, and the third for the VIPs. It was the first time that my people and close relatives had seen such a large number of items served.

Thus, two new members had been added to our family, now living in Walker Town, in the space of a few days.

Between 1970 and 1980, many changes took place in our family.

Marriage was a new chapter in my life, a new milestone. My father-in-law's influence had helped us in getting Narsing Rao and Anjiah transferred to the city. At first, it was suffocating for me to attend the frequent dinners hosted by my in-laws' friends – I was unused to such socializing.

The joint family soon began to break up, with each brother establishing his own family. In a few months' time, Anjiah decided to live separately with his wife, and they moved into a house of their own. He was – and is – a perfect gentleman and my father's favourite son. He was very attached to the family and had few friends, and was dependent on my father before he got married. My sister in law Rukmani was – and is – an efficient housewife, and ran her house well; Anjiah had to worry about little other than his profession. Their relationship is still such that they are almost inseparable.

Anjiah taught zoology to Telugu-medium students, and he proved to be a good teacher. He was a man contented with himself, and in spite of his brothers' advice to go for research in his subject, he did not make the attempt. He was an easy-going man; and when he finally retired, it was as the principal of the Government City College.

After Anjiah moved out, we moved to a smaller house in Bhoiguda. A couple of years later, Narsing Rao too decided to move – he had a son by this time. This left Balraj and me with Laxman and my parents. Soon after, though, Balraj too decided to move into his railway quarters at Rifle Range, leaving my wife, my first child, my parents, my youngest brother Laxman and me to live together. After the birth of my second daughter in 1977, we moved to the MLA quarters, where my mother-in-law had quarters allotted to her since she was a member of the legislative council. It was around this time that my mother, a chronic diabetic, began to need regular medical attention, and I would frequently take her to the doctor.

Abbasayulu was in deep trouble after leaving the railway job; for the job he was doing at Satyamma College he was paid inadequately, and irregularly at that. He, however, did not lose hope, and worked for his MPhil degree. My sister-in-law was a great strength to him, doing odd jobs to help maintain the family. Although I felt sorry for my brother, I was not able to help him financially – we had taken loans for the weddings, and were trying to repay them. Abbasayulu became a lecturer in Osmania University and from this point on, there was no turning back in my brother's career. He went on to become the first doctorate and the first professor in our family.

When, in the mid-1970s, he went to present a paper at an international seminar held in Australia, my father was in tears: the son for whom he had envisioned the role of a stationmaster had moved so far ahead in life that he was now flying to another country to present a paper! I was greatly excited too – my brother's journey had not been smooth; it had been an uphill task, in which he had remained strong and resolute. The airport itself was a new experience for all of us: in those days, one could view flights taking off or landing from the terrace of the airport, and I watched my brother leave.

Two of my daughters, Madhavi and Aradhana, were born when we were still in Bhoiguda, and the third, Jyoti Sree, was born after we moved to the MLA quarters. My parents wished for a baby boy every time my wife was with child, but each time they were disappointed.

Life was good in the MLA quarters. Madhavi started her studies at St Ann's School in Secunderabad. My father was her best friend, taking her to school each day; he enjoyed listening to her speak to her friends in convent English. After dropping her at school, he would visit one or the other of his sons in different places, walking everywhere. My daughter loved her grandfather. She would share whatever she had with her taata. She took special care of her grandfather, reminding me to get local cigars for him.

I did not enjoy living away from my brothers. I loved our joint family set-up. I now think that the joint family system is a failure when members have individual earnings and individual interests, and also when they have a huge inheritance. In our case, there was no wealth except the education our father had given us. In a joint family, the break-up starts when a person has children. The person with most income wants his children to have the most of everything; and in the joint family set-up, he wishes to contribute to the family what others contribute, and no more. Each individual who earns more money begins to save for himself and his children. Our family, when it had been a joint one, had been no exception.

In the early days of my marriage, my mother-in-law insisted that we employ a maid. This was a new phenomenon for us, and seemed strange, for we were used to doing our own work. We were actually hesitant to instruct the servant we appointed. My parents were uneasy with the arrangement and were confused as to how to behave in the presence of the servant. The idea of a maid was not new to my wife, though, and she was glad to have someone to help her.

The decade 1970–79 brought a lot of change in the identities of the individual families too. Studying in convent schools, the children, the second-generation learners, were at par with any middle-class family. There was no need for them to apply for a fee concession at school, and they had no Dalit identity as far as their school life was concerned. They competed with higher-caste students without knowing what caste was.

My parents had been living with me for more than four years when my mother began to feel that they were becoming a burden to me; they felt that none of my other brothers seemed to be thinking of them.

'Son, speak to your brothers; should we always stay with you? Is it not also their responsibility to take care of us?' my mother said one day, while I was preparing for my class the next day. She said this with a serious look. I thought that perhaps something had gone wrong, and that she was offended by something that I or my wife had done.

'Amma, is anything wrong? Is it something I've done, or your daughter-in-law?'

'No, Son, that's not it.'

'What is it, then? Are you unhappy staying with me?'

'No, Son, but there are four more brothers whose responsibility it is to take care of their old parents.'

'Oh, Mother, don't worry! Had I been your only son, wouldn't you have lived with me?'

'That's different. We have four other sons who are earning, and you have a wife who needs constant medical care due to her chronic bronchitis; I too need medical care – it is a strain on you, my son.'

'Mother, it is fine. I don't need to call any of my brothers. But if you want to, you may: I will only say, Father and you will never be a burden to me, just as my children are no burdens to me!' I was getting emotional and my eyes were moist.

My mother embraced me and sobbed while my father watched us silently. He became grave and agreed that my mother was right.

One Sunday, all of us gathered at my eldest brother Balraj's house at the behest of my father, the same small house that we had lived in until we finished our school. Those times, the school days, the way we lived in this small house – those memories were reeling in my head. I was uneasy and very uncomfortable, for I felt that the issue to be discussed was shameful. A discussion on how we should take care of our parents was uncalled for, in my opinion. I had tried to persuade Father against the idea, but he was adamant. None of my brothers had felt that taking care of our parents was an issue when we were living together, and I did not want my parents to live by turns in our houses. Even the thought of sharing the 'burden' of one's parents was shameful; it was not like sharing inherited property. My parents, who had strived hard to give us the best education possible, often going half-starved themselves, who had refused to let us work in the lowest jobs even when the family finances were not in great shape, were now asking us how we would share their burden.

Narsing Rao and Anjiah sat looking silently at each other, and at their wives. Balraj and Abbasayulu were discussing the issue.

'Peddanna, it's not fair to keep our parents any more with Satti. He has small children and his wife does not keep good health.'

'That is alright, I'll keep them with me,' said Balraj.

'No, we don't want to stay with anyone. Install us in a separate house.' My father meant every word.

'No, Father, we won't let you live separately. Mother needs attention at this age,' said Abbasayulu.

'Let us live with the eldest one, then; but all of you must help him, as he has a big family.' My mother preferred this house next to mine. Her preference was for her eldest daughter-in-law Pochamma, who had seen the family through many troubled times. They had had a long association and she understood my mother well.

My father then demanded that each of us pay Balraj two hundred rupees on the first of each month without being asked for it. 'It is not property I am distributing, my sons, but I'm asking you to share our living expenses.' My father broke down.

I shall always remember the scene with the greatest agony, and I can never excuse myself for having allowed it. My brothers were sad too. Everyone was weeping inwardly, and all of us asked my parents to stay with them. A father who had raised his children with the utmost care and with the single-minded purpose of giving them the best education was now asking his own children for his living expenses: it shook my mind and body, and I felt ashamed and helpless. But in spite of my repeated requests not to leave me, my father said, embracing me, 'Bidda, Satti, we have been with you for the past four years. Let us be with anna now. We will visit you frequently, whenever I miss my granddaughters.' That gave me some solace.

In 1979, there was a serious financial crisis in my college. The management had no money to pay salaries. This situation was a result of mismanagement by the college administration. There was a strike by teachers and other staff, and the management was thinking of replacing the principal. They wanted me to be the principal. I discussed the offer with my close friends Rama Rao and Subba Rao. Although Subba Rao spoke little, his thinking was always clear and unbiased. Whether one liked it or not, he was always frank in expressing his opinion. Rama Rao, the closer friend of the two, was more biased towards me; we would often sit at either Koti or Abid's, gossiping in the evenings for hours together. Our friendship has been the strongest of all. Both my friends thought that I should take up the offer. Ultimately, with my friends' coaxing and on the advice of my father-in-law, I took up the position of principal. At thirty-three, I was probably the youngest man occupying the top post there.

Being newly established, there were several problems in the college. With inadequate support from the management, it was a daily challenge to run the college. But I worked hard. I obtained the necessary funds from the government, and tackled issues using a humane approach rather than trying to be authoritarian. Rama Rao was with me through thick and thin during this period. The college staff consisted mostly of Brahmins, or people from the Kamma and Reddy castes – all higher castes – and I was a Dalit. However, I had no problems with my Brahmin colleagues; they were friendly, reliable and helpful, right to the end of my service.

There was heartburn, though, with a Reddy. Once, I was sitting in the physics lab, talking to Rama Rao and another friend from the neighbouring college – my namesake and also a Madiga like me, Satyanarayana. Satyanarayana was anxious to tell me something. When Rama Rao left us to explain an experiment to a student, I took him to my office. I thought he was going to tell me something confidential.

'The other day, Reddy, your botany lecturer, came to me,' he whispered.

'And?' I asked impatiently.

He looked grim, and I asked him the reason for his seriousness.

'Do you know what he said?'

I was curious, 'What?'

'He said that he is forced to work under a Madiga. He did not know that I too am a Madiga!'

'What was your reply?' I was angry; my face had turned red as I tried to control myself.

'Do you think that I kept quiet? I took off my sandal and tried to give him a slap, but somebody stopped me!'

I offered him a glass of water, which seemed to cool him down a little. 'Friend, do not take this seriously,' I said. 'After all, in this caste-ridden society, antagonism and intolerance by the higher castes does remain. And he is a Reddy; he expects us to remain at his feet. But now, we have a strong weapon: education. Let us use it.' Although I too had been angered, I kept my cool.

'No, friend. I would advise you to be careful about him.'

'He cannot pluck a single hair of mine. Do not worry.'

I came to know the true colours of casteism through this man. Reddy was polite to me, but hostile behind my back. He would scheme to put me in situations that would force me to quit office. Once, he tried to implicate me in an examination scandal involving me and a student leader, using the latter as the weapon to get to me. But his plan boomeranged, and he was in deep trouble. The student leader was powerful, and made Reddy's life miserable, even chasing him in the streets. For more than three years, this student caused Reddy sleepless nights, and although he approached many teachers' organizations and made representations to the chief minister, all of it was futile. When the time came for his retirement, he was apprehensive that I might create problems in sending out his pension papers, but when I simply processed the papers as I would have for any other employee, he was taken by surprise and ultimately confessed.

Another incident that disturbed me was when a library assistant made the comment that being a Madiga, I was not fit to lead the staff. I was troubled at this comment, but not angry with him; it was upper-caste arrogance, the varna system that made him speak thus. No constitutional safeguards so far had really helped the hapless Dalits; they still remained excluded, segregated and untouchable in free India. The mindset of upper-caste Hindus had not changed much in spite of the relentless efforts of Dr B.R. Ambedkar, the saviour of the oppressed, who had said, while drafting the constitution, 'I came into the Constituent Assembly with no greater aspiration than to safeguard the interests of scheduled castes.' I was reminded of this statement, and decided to teach the boy a lesson. I posted him at my office door, where he had to sit on a stool all day, and enter my room and take orders whenever I rang the bell. This continued for more than six months, until he realized why I was fit to be his boss. He was finally repentant, and fell at my feet one day, asking for pardon. I was happy that he had realized his mistake.

※

My life took another turn when my mother-in-law's term as member of the legislative council ended. We left the MLA quarters and moved to Kishanguda, a village outside the city of Hyderabad, where she had a poultry farm and rice mill. Kishanguda was a small hamlet with only about a hundred inhabitants, most of them gowdas or toddy tappers. There was little in terms of untouchability and other caste-based social restrictions here. For one thing, the village was close to the city and was influenced by urban ways, and for another, my mother-in-law, though a Dalit, was a former minister, and she commanded a lot of respect in this region. Staying at Kishanguda, I found myself involved willy-nilly in the maintenance of the poultry farm and the rice mill, and this was not to my liking.

I had to admit my daughter Madhavi to the hostel at St Ann's School, as the distance was too great for her to travel each day. For myself, I had to cover the considerable distance of fifteen miles on scooter to reach the college. It became a rather stressful and physically exhausting routine. Being respectful of my mother-in-law, I had accepted her suggestion without consideration for my family. I knew her temperament, and found her good at heart, but also short-tempered and intolerant of anyone who disagreed with her. I also thought that a difference of opinion would create a rift between us. She talked to me about leading an independent life, and would affectionately call me 'Beta'. She even tried to influence me to quit the job and enter business, but this proposal did not appeal to me. Although I was against it, I would hear her out, without committing myself. Now, I began to feel resentful, as if she was taking over my family.

Neither my parents nor my brothers were happy with me. They were worried about my family as well as the long commute my new address meant for me. I too felt that I was stuck in the situation because I had been unable to refuse my mother-in-law. I continued to visit my parents often, and on one such visit my father took me to task.

'Son, how are my grandchildren and daughter-in-law?' began my father.

'They are well, Father,' I smiled.

'Bidda, why have you moved so far away when we are all here?' he continued.

While I was still trying to answer him, he went on, 'Son, it appears as if you have surrendered yourself to your rich in-laws and are living with them.'

'No Father, I was just helping them ...'

'Who would believe that? I gave you a good education to enable you to live on your own with dignity.'

I had no answer; I could understand his feelings.

'Bidda, don't be under somebody's shelter when you are capable of giving shelter to others. Make your parents proud, for they raised you keeping themselves half-starved; make them proud of you.' Father was getting emotional, but he was right; my parents had worked relentlessly for my well-being and their efforts had made me what I was. My dependence on my in-laws hurt their feelings.

'Father, don't be angry. I will shift to the city shortly. Your granddaughters need schooling and I intend to admit them to convent schools.'

He and my mother, who had been sitting by my side all through this conversation, were happy to hear this.

My father had not been rich and never owned a house, but he enabled his sons to reach a position where they could make their fortunes. He did not compromise on his convictions. He had not read or heard Ambedkar, but his thoughts matched that man's. 'You must abolish slavery yourselves. It is disgraceful to live at the cost of one's self-respect. Self-respect is a most vital factor in life. Without it man is a mere cipher. To live worthily with self-respect one has to overcome difficulties. It is out of hard and ceaseless struggle alone that one derives strength, confidence and recognition,' Dr Ambedkar had said while addressing a huge rally of women at Yeola, Nasik, on 13 October 1935. I remember my father's words, 'Bidda, do not bend yourself before anyone. No matter whether you are starving, your pride should never be mortgaged.' He may not have been a scholar, but he believed in self-respect and was himself a highly disciplined man.

My fourth daughter, Nischala, was born when we were in Kishanguda. My two other girls were also growing up and I was concerned about their education. When my mother-in-law suggested admitting them to a nearby school, I told her that I would not, as I felt that they should go to good schools. It was time for me to move to the city again. She suggested admitting them into the best residential schools possible, but I was against the idea. She was unhappy, but I was resolute and did not compromise. I did, however, accept staying on rent in a close relative's house so that she might visit the children frequently.

In April 1980, we moved back to the city. It was a great relief for me, and my parents were happy. The person who was made very happy by this was my father, who frequently visited us so he could play with his granddaughters. Madhavi came back home, and Aradhana and Jyoti Sree began kindergarten. They now had a full-time nanny. Life became comfortable, though not luxurious. I had a telephone at home – another first in our family. Soon enough, a refrigerator, a dining table, a sofa set and a television also became part of our furnishings. One wonderful memory I carry from those days is of Father sitting on a sofa reading *Chandamama*, and my mother teasing him. Mother was very happy too, and I began to take care of her health again, occasionally taking her to doctors to monitor her blood glucose levels. I wished I could purchase a car to take my parents and children around, but my desire remained unfulfilled as long as my father was alive.

Abbasayulu, Narsing Rao and Anjiah were well-settled as lecturers in different colleges. People marvelled at how a single family had produced four lecturers. Life was good now in every family. I began to observe the slow cultural transformation of each family towards Sanskritization. In our joint family, Durgamma thottela (Durgamma's cradle) and Narsimha Swamy, a ferocious lion-headed god, were the only deities we had ever known, and I had never seen my parents worshipping them ritually. We had a simple process: my father would offer food to Goddess Durgamma – rice and mutton, and sometimes a bottle of liquor, pray briefly, and then enjoy drinking and eating the offerings. There were no such things as fasting, offering flowers, or making special vegetarian dishes and offering them – untouched and untasted by others – to the gods. But now I would find pictures of gods and goddesses like Saraswati, Lakshmi, Ganapati and Venkateshwara in our families. In some of my brothers' houses, a holy tulsi plant was also placed according to the rules of Vastu. In fact, Narsing Rao and Anjiah engaged in daily worship with the ritualistic ringing of a bell.

My own house was influenced by Arya Samaj customs. My father-in-law, a staunch Arya Samaji, taught the Gayatri Mantram to my children, and on weekends they would sit and do havan, reciting mantras. I was hardly interested, and my children did not develop an interest either. They saw this ritual as imposed, and did it only to satisfy my father-in-law. Individual families also began to visit pilgrim centres like Tirupati, Vijayawada, Srisailam and others.

I see it as a privilege that I was able to provide my mother comfort when we went to a couple of pilgrim centres. Mother wished to go to Tirupati, and she asked me to take her. I made the necessary arrangements. She was travelling in a sleeper second-class coach for the first time and was impressed with the comfort of travel. She was very happy and thought it to be a luxurious journey. My children were excited and argued over who would sit at the window, reminding me of the days when my father used to take us on those long tours. I had arranged for a cab from Tirumala to get us to the hill temple, along with arranging the accommodation, as well as a special darshan, and my mother thought it all perfectly lavish.

'Ayya, I am so happy. It was a special darshan for us! But I'm afraid you've spent too much money on it all.'

This was the second time during the trip that she had mentioned the expenses and I said to her, 'Mother, please do not talk of money hereafter; what I need is your comfort.'

She did not bring up the issue again, and enjoyed the rest of the pilgrimage.

On another trip, I took her to visit the temple of our family deity, Durgamma. We went to the Kanaka Durga temple in Vijayawada, and she was extremely happy. That trip was made in the summer, and we booked ourselves into a good hotel which had air-conditioning too. Needless to say, Mother was thrilled with the comforts.

It was 1982; I was in Delhi attending an orientation course at the National Institute of Educational Planning and Administration (NIEPA). About fifty principals of colleges from across the country were participating in the three-week course. It was an opportunity for me to get exposed to some innovative ideas in educational administration. I was the youngest among the participants and the course director, Dr Sharma, addressed me as the youngest college principal in India. It made me feel both happy and somehow important. The course was designed to help principals in the administration of their colleges. Some senior principals were of the opinion that they did not have much to learn as they had already learnt a great deal from their experience. I, however, was keen to learn as much as possible; I was sure that it would help me in the future.

There was a debate on the subject of emancipation of scheduled caste and scheduled tribe students, and the affirmative actions a principal could take to achieve this goal. It was an interesting and important topic, during which I came to know the attitude of caste Hindus towards this section of students. Instead of discussing how best the students' grievances could be addressed and their socio-economic sufferings relieved, or how the social ills of untouchability and segregation could be removed, there was a deviation from the subject and everyone started discussing how long the reservations should continue. The antagonism was clear. None of the heads of institutions was even *thinking* in favour of reservations for Dalit students. One principal made a derogatory remark, 'Aap kitni bhi chhoot de, ye harijans sudharne vale nahi hain. No matter what reservations you provide and however long you extend it, these Harijans are never going to get any better. Their children attend colleges simply to receive the scholarship money.' I could see upper-caste arrogance in his words; he had not made a single affirmative suggestion and was showing his contempt and hatred against students from the scheduled castes and tribes. I could not restrain myself any more and said, 'I strongly protest against the remarks made against Dalit students. They are derogatory and insulting, and if this is the attitude of the principal, I wonder how his unfortunate and neglected students can expect any social justice.' My face had turned red, and everyone was stunned at my outburst. Even the director looked apologetic as he had kept quiet even when so much was being spoken against the constitutional rights guaranteed to the oppressed, and this despite the fact that the chosen topic deviated from the subject for discussion. I then took half an hour and quoted Jyotiba Phule and Ambedkar extensively. Mahatma Phule had strongly opposed a system where Brahmins and other higher-caste people taught Sudras and other lower castes, and now, the attitude of such teachers proved him correct. I quoted Jyotirao Phule, 'Let there be schools for the Sudras in every village; but away with all Brahmin school-masters! The Sudras are the life and sinews of the country, and it is to them alone and not to the Brahmins that the government must ever look to tide them over their difficulties, financial as well as political.'

My outburst caused me to be noticed by every participant principal, and I subsequently received attention from everyone. There was no Dalit present in the programme except me, and it came as a surprise to everyone that I was a Dalit. Had they known about it, the discussion might not have been so intense and forceful against Dalits. The person who spoke against the issue apologized to me after the debate.

The programme itself did prove useful to me, since I had relatively little experience in my service as principal, and this interaction with many heads of educational institutions from all over the country provided an opportunity to learn many new things.

When I returned home, my children were overjoyed to see me. It was the first time I had been away from them, and each of my daughters was vying to sit on my lap. They were all talking to me at the same time, and trying to grab my attention. They wanted to see what I had brought for them, but at the same time they did not want to let go of me, and held me tight. It took a while for them to even allow me to go take a bath!

The next day, I visited my parents. I was anxious as my mother had been waiting for an examination by the endocrinologist.

'How are you, my son; when did you come?' My mother was happy to see me. Father was curious about the bag I was holding. I brought out a sweater for my mother, and a branded local cigar box and whisky bottle for my father. They were overjoyed. Father invited his old friends over to share the drink the very next day; this was his way of telling his friends that his sons were getting foreign liquor for him, and branded local cigars!

It was late in the evening, and I was still in my office, when a peon entered. 'Sir, your father is here.'

I wondered why Father had to see me at that time. As he entered, I noticed that although he was smiling, he looked tired, and his clothes were soiled. My father, who always went out in a spotless white dhoti and creaseless white shirt. I was shaken to see him in such a condition.

'Father, are you well?' I asked, touching his forehead. He was not running a temperature. He sat quietly and replied slowly, 'I'm okay.'

'How is Mother?' I asked anxiously, although he kept calm. Suddenly I remembered the date: it was the fifteenth of the month, and I hadn't sent them the monthly amount that was due to them on the tenth of every month. I wept within myself, and though my father did not say anything, I understood what he wanted to say. I realized that he wanted to tell me something, but couldn't spell it out. He never spoke against any of his sons in the presence of another. I understood, however, and wound up my work and took my father out shopping on my scooter. I bought him three sets of clothes – dhotis, shirts and undergarments. He was happy but hesitant to take them. I understood his dilemma, and told him that I would bring them to him the next day, when I visited.

Of all my brothers, Balraj had the largest family, consisting of four sons and three daughters. His children were the only ones to have attended the railway school. After the break-up of the joint family, he had had to face tough times. His oldest daughter had been married when he and I still lived together. He had left us when Madhavi was born. Each brother had left the joint family after some sort of disagreement or altercation, but not Balraj. He had chosen to leave because he did not want to burden me when he already had a house available for his use. We never had any disagreement. When I visited his house, I would feel as if I was in my old house and my mind would take me back to the days I spent here – my childhood, my school days. Every part of this house and the surroundings would remind me afresh of past memories and of the deep attachment within my family. This house played a significant role in shaping the future of each one of us; this was where we read under flickering kerosene lamps in the days when we had no electricity and completed our school education. Balraj still treated me with the same love and affection as when I had been a boy, and my sister-in-law would never allow me to leave without having me eat something. The children loved me and we were very close to one another.

Balraj had, after twenty years, once again taken shelter in this house when the joint family broke up. He had stayed with us until after the completion of our education, employment and marriage. It was indeed a long period that he lived with his younger brothers; he had helped them grow in their education, obtain good employment and better living conditions, and had then come back to his earlier position and quarters. With his seven children, it was tough for him to maintain his family. Nevertheless, he was able to make two of his sons engineers, and a daughter a lecturer. Even after we separated, my brother would consult me before taking any major decision.

Balraj still maintained some of the traditions we observed when we were a joint family. He would invite all of us to his house once a year on Dussehra, and the whole family would gather in his small house to have a feast after the Durgamma Puja. This was the only time in the year when all of Baliah's children and grandchildren got together at one place to celebrate, and it was a long-awaited event. It was great fun for the children too. My mother would be delighted and busy with her twenty-five grandchildren; she met some of them only occasionally, and one could see her trying to recall some of their names. Unlike other children, my daughter Madhavi would sit on her grandfather's lap and both would often be engaged in deep discussion. She was attached to my father, and would insist that he come and stay with us. My father, on his part, would be very happy and curious to hear her speak in English. It was also an occasion for us to sit together gossiping till late in the evening, while my father and older brothers shared drinks. Heavy drinking would sometimes cause us to end up in petty quarrels where one or the other, often my two elder brothers, or my older brother-in-law, would claim credit for something in the joint family. My father would have to pacify them at such times.

Once he became a reader at the university, Abbasayulu had no financial problems. He soon purchased a house at Medi Bawi, in Sitaphalmandi.

Abbasayulu's eldest daughter, Tara, was a beautiful girl who behaved strangely sometimes; at such times she had to be taken to a psychiatrist. She had studied only up to the tenth standard, and was now married to a bank employee. It was deeply shocking for us to learn one day that she had jumped into a well when no one was at home and committed suicide. My brother was still as stone, his eyes red and dry, as if there were no tears inside him. But when her body was pulled out of the well, he fell on me, sobbing; I too burst out crying. She looked fresh and quiet, as if she were asleep. My sister-in-law fell unconscious each time she looked at her daughter's dead body. The most beautiful girl from our family had left us, leaving behind her ten-month-old infant daughter.

I took to visiting Abbasayulu and my sister-in-law frequently. My brother decided not to keep the child with them, but to send her to her father, and I supported him, although my sister-in-law was not happy with this decision.

Tara's death was a blow to my father, and it showed in the state of his health. Unlike Mother, Father had never needed to visit the doctor; he did not worry about death either, saying it was a certainty, and the only two things he needed daily were liquor and local cigars. Now, old age was visible on his face. His strong muscles became loose and began to hang, and he lost some teeth too. Though my parents lived with my eldest brother, Father would frequently visit each of us. Earlier, he would go everywhere on foot, covering long distances, but now he began to have joint pains and preferred to remain at home. The sudden decline of his health was a matter of concern to everyone in the family; my two sisters spent much of their time helping my mother.

When I saw him next, three months had passed, and I was shocked when I saw him. He had taken a fall in the bathroom, and was now walking with the help of a stick. He needed constant help, was nearly bedridden, and needed help even to use the bathroom. I could not hold back my tears. My mother led me out of the room saying, 'Don't weep, my son, your father is fine.' But she was wiping her own tears as she said this.

'Mother, why don't you come to me?'

'No, Son, your brother's feelings will be hurt. We are okay here.' For her, each son was as good as the other.

'Son, I hate this kind of living; I need help even to get up,' my father said as I helped him to a chair. His eyes were damp, and in his unshaven face, his big eyes were now sunk deep into their sockets. He had poor eyesight and had lost most of his teeth.

'Don't worry, Father, you will be alright,' I said as I placed his long stick beside his chair.

My father, a strong man in his youth, was no longer the same. As all else, his body had had to yield to time and circumstances. There was a time when he could lift bags weighing a quintal with ease; even body builders and wrestlers were afraid of his physique. Today he was sitting helplessly in a chair, holding a stick. A man who had fought adversity his whole life was struggling while his sons were busy with their lives and could hardly find time to see their father. He cursed old age for making him dependent on others. To me, it seemed that everyone was tired of looking after him.

I had taken up my doctoral research at this time, despite the busy administrative work. The work was not moving beyond a particular stage, for the experiments I needed to conduct required certain specific conditions. I was worried if I would be able to conduct them successfully and was waiting for guidance from my friend Dr Chandrapal – my classmate in postgraduate studies and now in the Department of Chemistry at Osmania University – who was my research supervisor.

'Sir, I have completed most of what the experiment required. A little is left and ...'

'I know that, Satyanarayana. I shall ask Devi Prasad to help you complete your work, but you will have to go to Nizam College.'

The laboratory in Nizam College had the facilities required for my experiments.

'I don't mind, Sir. I shall do the rest of the work at Nizam College,' I said.

My friend was happy that the work was nearing completion, though he himself was busy with administrative work and found it hard to spare the time.

Devi Prasad was young and had great respect for me, and assured me that my work would be completed in a few months. I was happy; I completed the work as far as possible by going as early as five each morning to Nizam College and conducting the experiments in the lab. But after writing the first chapter of the thesis, to my surprise, I found a sudden change in him. He began to avoid me when I visited him to show him my draft. He was also a Dalit. I sometimes had to wait at his door for half an hour before he would come out. If I was late by even a bit, he would be unavailable. This was humiliating to me; it was apparent that he did not want me to hold a high position in a college. Finally, he sent word, after nearly ten months, that he could not spare his time. I was frustrated and made up my mind to give up my pursuit of the PhD.

One evening I was sitting with Dr Rama Rao over a coffee when he asked, 'What happened to your thesis?'

'I have decided to give up the work,' I said in a low voice.

'Are you crazy? You want to give up your work at this stage?'

'What can I do? That fellow has been indifferent and the other day he said he could no longer spare his time.'

My friend was upset. He really wanted me to complete my doctoral work. He had completed his own doctoral work a long time ago, and since then had been after me to take it up. He had heard some adverse comments from people, to the effect that I was just posing to be doing research, and he was angry.

'Why is that man not helping you? He is also a Dalit, after all,' he said angrily.

'Well, if I complete my research, I would become a threat to him.'

'Oh! Let him go to hell! Approach your friend Dr Chandrapal and let him decide. But you shouldn't give up at this stage. People will laugh at you, at *us*. Many are already of the opinion that you are incapable of completing the work.' He was serious.

'Very well, Ramu, I shall discuss the matter with Chandrapal.'

'Yes, do it tomorrow; don't waste any more time.'

We sat there for some more time, discussing the issue.

The next day, I visited Chandrapal at his house early in the morning. He knew about the situation and was upset, 'Friend, I am sorry for what has happened. I did not expect this from Devi Prasad. Let's forget him; I assure you that we shall complete this work at the earliest.'

'Thank you,' I said. 'I had actually started to think that I should give up the work.'

'No, no. How can that be, you have almost *completed* the work! I shall see to it that your thesis is completed without any further loss of time.' He regretted what had happened, and repeatedly asked me not to lose heart or momentum. He promised that we would work together, and that I would get my doctoral degree in about six months' time.

I had hoped to complete my doctorate while my father was alive, but that was one desire I could not fulfil.

On 13 July 1983, the life of Yelukati Ramaswamy, better known as Yelukati Baliah, came to an end. The man who had taught his sons discipline, made them tough and uncompromising, enabled them to reach the highest possible heights in education, and given them a good standing in society breathed his last. He had set an example for many Dalit families and was popular among not only Dalit communities but among all railway employees from Secunderabad to Kazipet. He was no social reformer and had not read Ambedkar, but he fought social evils at his own level and was uncompromising in his fight. He had refused to be subservient to anyone throughout his life, and had therefore commanded respect even from those who belonged to the higher castes.

At my eldest brother's house, where my father's body lay, my mother was wailing, sitting at his feet; she had lost her lifelong companion, the person with whom she had spent more than fifty years. They had travelled a long journey as they raised their children, sharing the heavy burden of their large family; and now she was cursing him for leaving her behind. He had breathed his last in her arms and left this world with no more desires: his children were well settled; he had seen his grandchildren and had enjoyed playing with them. Everyone was weeping and there was nobody to console us. My mother broke down afresh on seeing the rest of her children; Madhavi sat close to Father's dead body, sobbing; the other children were weeping too.

We brothers sat in a corner, trying to talk about the funeral. Wiping his tears, Balraj said, 'Let's wait. Akka has to come from Nekkonda; I have sent word to her.'

'The train reaches at four. Let's complete the other formalities,' said Abbasayulu.

People started pouring in from different places – from Kazipet to Secunderabad railway stations. A big crowd gathered to mourn Father's death. Railway officials placed a wreath on my father's dead body – a rare honour not generally given to ordinary employees. The whole colony was grief-stricken, and every resident came to meet my eldest brother and offer their condolences.

Traditionally, five elders (close relatives) go to get the materials needed for the bier; they go for a drink before purchasing the material. A small fire is lit in front of the house where the deceased person's body is kept. This fire would be used to cook some rice in an earthen pot, and to boil water to give a final bath to the dead. Four people carry the bier on their shoulders to the crematorium as part of a solemn procession;

people dance to the beat of drums and the eldest son holds an earthen pot as he walks in front of the dead body. In Dalit and Sudra communities, women accompany men in the funeral procession. In earlier days, untouchables used to bury their dead, but now, they too consign their dead to the flames.

It was six in the evening when the funeral procession left Balraj's house. It was my father's last journey, and there was a huge crowd. The procession moved slowly as we brothers took turns to carry our father on our shoulders. A dozen Madigas beat drums, and a few people danced to the beats, stopping the procession here and there. It took two hours to reach the crematorium at Mettuguda, where a jangam, belonging to an affiliate caste of the Madiga, performed the last rites and rituals.

I know my father to have been a great man in his own way, and it is in his memory that I write this book. It is my tribute to him.

Acknowledgements

I would like to thank all the people who helped me in bringing out this book, a family biography. I am greatly indebted to my grandfather Narsiah, my father Baliah and my mother Narsamma, without whose oral contributions this book could not have been written. My thanks are also due to my good friend and senior journalist, Mallepalli Lakshmiah, whose constant reminders and gentle coaxing helped me complete this book. I acknowledge my debt to Ms Gita Ramaswamy, who took a keen interest in my script and read it through in a very, very short time. Her encouragement gave me great strength, and without her help this script would not have reached the publishers. I thank Ms Sheel Parekh, who edited the draft, for her total involvement in the scrutiny of the text and her attention to detail. I pay my respects to S.R. Sankaran, IAS (retd), for writing the foreword to this book. Finally, I thank my wife, Gayatri, and my children and grandchildren, without whose help and inspiration I could not have written this book.